Black Wall Street DotCom

Black Wall Street DotCom

How to Build a Thriving Black Business Using the Laws of the Universe

Marye Dean, Esq.

Published by Game Changer Publishing

ISBN: 978-1-7370407-8-1

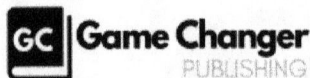

GC | **Game Changer**
PUBLISHING

www.GameChangerPress.com

DEDICATION

DeShrondra Norris
#ShonShine

DOWNLOAD YOUR FREE GIFT

Read This First

Just to say thank you for buying and reading my book, I would like to give you a free gift from BlackWallStreet.com!

To Download Now, Visit:

www.BlackWallStreet.com/freegift

Black Wall Street DotCom

How to Build a Thriving Black Business
Using the Laws of the Universe

Marye Dean, Esq.
TheWallStreetLawyer.com

GC **Game Changer**
PUBLISHING

www.GameChangerPress.com

Black Wall Street DotCom

For the early part of the 20th century, Black Wall Street was one of the most affluent African American communities in the United States of America. According to Hannibal Johnson, author of *Black Wall Street: From Riot to Renaissance in Tulsa's Historic Greenwood District*, it was O.W. Gurley who owned the first black business there. "He had a vision to create something for black people by black people."

Other prominent black entrepreneurs followed suit. J.B. Stradford, a lawyer and activist who was born into slavery, built a 55-room luxury hotel bearing his name–the largest black-owned hotel in the country. An outspoken businessman, Stradford believed that blacks had a better chance of economic progress if they pooled their resources.

I agree.

It was said that within Black Wall Street, every dollar would change hands 19 times before it left the community. Black Wall Street thrived as the epicenter of African American business and culture until it was burned to the ground on May 31, 1921.

One hundred years later, **BlackWallStreet.com** was born.

Welcome to the new Black Wall Street.

Marye Dean, Esq.
TheWallStreetLawyer.com

Repeat After Me:

Abundance is my birthright. I release the narrative that I must struggle to have abundance. Part of my soul makeup is having the keen awareness that I am full of abundance and am most fulfilled when I serve my community because love begins at home. I realize that the hardest lessons on earth serve my highest good, and I work diligently to heal as I transmute the energy of trauma into triumph. When I make decisions and take action using my specific strategy for success, I align my natural energetic structure on a subconscious level to allow for flow. When I operate in my truth and grace, abundance is my natural manifestation.

Ase'

Marye Dean, Esq. - TheWallStreetLawyer.com

Occupy Wall Street circa 2011

Table of Contents

"You lack nothing. Use what I gave you."

~ God

From Playing Business Dress Up to Leading a Worthwhile Company

I am Christiane Holbrook. You've probably never heard of me because my team and I love working in the background. We quietly strategize and market for several huge-thinking, mission-driven, remarkable entrepreneurs like Marye Dean, Esq. @TheWallStreetLawyer.com. But this is not about my business. This is about my experience with the **LIFT** material you are about to discover in this book. For about 25 years, I watched my ex-husband build a multimillion-dollar company from scratch. While I was passionately involved in the creative aspects of that growth, when it came to the dry, problematic aspects of running a business (things like numbers, contracts, legal protection, taxes, etc.), I shied away. I left it to him. I ignored and dismissed it.

A few years later, we got divorced, and because of a detrimental prenuptial agreement, I could not share in any of the wealth we created. Still, I continued ignoring any significant legal or financial aspects of life. Luckily, I had just enough capital to start my own business. With more than 25 years of business-building experience, I looked forward to showing the world what I was capable of. I created a beautiful website. I sounded confident. I hired staff. I did what I saw every successful coach and marketer do, but it was not enough. Deep down inside, I knew that how others saw me was not how I saw myself. Even though I was great at strategizing and marketing my own business, I never took the time to do what still felt hard. I never took the time to create a concrete business structure underneath my company.

Even though my business grew, I made money, and my clients loved me, I often still felt like an imposter incongruent with who I aspired to be. Here I was telling my clients that a magnetic brand was the essential foundation for business success while I consistently ignored the other corporate foundation pillars, the foundation Ms. Dean will patiently guide you through in this book. I don't want to take away the suspense, but I can assure you that working closely with Ms. Dean and her remarkable gifts while implementing the strong **LIFT** foundation you will learn about in this book will give you the same results it gave me; genuine confidence about my business, its long-term success, and with myself as a trustworthy business leader in my field. Because let's face it, in the past, I was only playing dress-up with my business.

I will always be grateful for the **LIFT** materials, which made the hard things so easy that I could finally face and master them, and with that, stop forever playing dress-up. I am grateful from the bottom of my heart for this material which helped me bring my business out of the shadow and into the light.

Christiane Holbrook,
CEO of Inspired Business Resources Incorporated

INTRODUCTION

The Game Changer

What you hold in your hands now is the result of nearly a million dollars' worth of education and on-the-job trial and failure. It began with three years at Georgetown University Law Center, more than six years of entrepreneurial experience, and some extremely expensive, painful missteps by my mentor, Alexis Neely, in addition to my 15 years of experience as an attorney and corporate consultant on Wall Street. I graduated from Thurgood Marshall School of Law, where I was taught "A lawyer who is not a social engineer is a social parasite." I've learned quite a bit over the years, and I am delighted to share my knowledge with you here in *Black Wall Street DotCom*.

Are you ready to finally hear the truth, dispelling the last of the genuinely taboo subjects? Here it is, and it is so taboo, your friends and colleagues do not talk about it. So taboo that there are no teleclasses or interviews about it. So taboo, you probably won't even find articles, blog posts, or much of anything about this topic on the internet. And because this topic is so taboo, it has become the elephant in the room. Why? Because it is the one thing that separates a real business owner who is making a lot of money with ease and grace using their gifts, talents, and services from those who have what I've heard referred to as an "imaginary business" or a "shadow business."

What is a shadow business? Have you ever heard the term, "Fake it until you make it?" A shadow business is not really a business at all. It's only pretending to be a business, like children playing dress-up with too-big clothes, so they keep falling to the floor. It's fun in the beginning, but keep it up for long and it starts to get frustrating and stressful. The worst part is that you see these businesses every day. They are the ones who have a great online or social media presence and appear to be helping a lot of people. But in reality, they are floundering along, not really making any money, and at risk of crumbling at the first sign of trouble. You may even have one of these businesses yourself. What is the biggest dirty secret of all? There are far more imaginary businesses out there than there are real ones. That probably would not be such a bad thing if they were not the ones we were constantly paying the most attention to.

I have been in the online entrepreneurial world for the past seven years of my legal career as TheWallStreetLawyer.com. Recently, I've been growing my business alongside some of the biggest names on the internet that you may have heard of, including Dr. Boyce Watkins and Alexis Neely, to name a few. Within a short period of time, I began privately coaching with Ms. Alexis Neely, revamping my practice to help me grow the kind of business and life that I deserved. She helped me launch my second business (In the Black Resources, LLC DBA Black Wall Street), which I grew to seven-figures within one year of meeting her. (As of the publication of this book I am still within my first year of working with Ms. Neely. I am speaking my business into existence, and you should be too!) Working with Alexis Neely is amazing. I was able to see her behind-the-scenes work as she revamped her business as well. What I saw gave me an insight into where I have been holding myself back for years, but in a way that I would not have imagined possible. On the flip side of that, I've watched several business owners go from solid seven-figure businesses into massive debt and loss. Over time, I discovered that I love to learn, and I learned to teach. All this time, as I've been learning from these amazing coaches and entrepreneurs online and observing these real-deal, serious entrepreneurs behind the scenes, I've also been distilling the greatest lessons so I could share them with you in this book to help you build a thriving black business. When it comes down to it, that is exactly what this book is all about–rebuilding Black Wall Street and creating black generational wealth. Real Black Power.

Often people who seem to be playing a big game are really not. It may look like they are on the surface, but in reality, they are playing very small. They are people who always look good, value their images very highly, and take great pains to maintain that image, but you have no idea what all that image is hiding underneath the surface, and sometimes neither do they. When the image is very strong, it is often masking a hidden underbelly, which we will come to discuss as the shadow.

This book is not just about how to legally set up your business, but it is also about all the other aspects of business that we often overlook–the insurance, finance, and tax systems that you need to truly be successful. As a Wall Street lawyer and entrepreneur I am in a unique position to hear about things that others do not–the disputes, financial crisis, drama, conflicts, and all of the other taboos of starting and running a business.

People talk to me about all of these things because they know I am not here to judge their experiences. And believe me, I have heard it all! I am not exaggerating when I say that this book could change your business and your life in ways that you could never have imagined! If you take these principles and apply them to your business, you could not only make a fortune, but you may also finally find your path to the deep down, never-before-felt freedom that you and your black family truly deserve.

Who am I, and why on earth should you invest your time and your money with me?

Chances are you've run into me somewhere, maybe on Instagram, Facebook, YouTube, or some of the work that I've been doing recently with Dr. Boyce Watkins on his platforms, or from the David Banner Podcast or any other names that you may know. Maybe you've read about me in *Forbes* or seen me on Fox News, ABC News, Fox Business, or CBS. What you may not know is that over the past 15 years of my legal career I helped several clients build big entrepreneurial business ventures from scratch, turning two of them into seven-figure businesses. I have also worked with many seven-figure business owners on Wall Street to help them redefine their business structures. The result is in the teachings that fill the pages of this book that relate to **LIFT**ing your business and life to a new level of awareness so you can become the inspired business leader you know deep down inside that you can be.

Are your life and business the way you want them to be right now? Are you happy with your relationships? The amount of money you are making? How much you are working? Your state of being on a daily basis, and the way that you feel? If you are happy with all of that, you can stop reading this book and go find something else to do with your precious, valuable time. If you are not, if you know things can be better and you want them to be, if you want to make more money, or if you are struggling with a difficult customer, a team member, or even your marriage or children, then keep reading because I am going to help you. You have your eyes and your awareness closed to something that is right in front of you. Learn to operate your business from a place of Supreme Awareness, and the world around you will change. That is my promise. That is my **Black Wall Street Guarantee**.

To Get In the Black, you must operate your business from a place of Supreme Awareness.

Let me be absolutely blunt here. You simply cannot continue to operate your business the way that you have been; it is just too much. You are on edge and you know it. In one way or another, you have felt the effects of America's racial tensions and the economic shakedown of 2020, and now you have a choice. You can see what's happening to you as a wake-up call, or you can continue to operate the way you have always operated in the same patterned, conditioned ways that have gotten so many business owners in trouble, feeling as if their business is built on a shaky foundation. Make no mistake about it; it very likely is.

Let's look at a couple of industries that woke up too late despite the serious warnings. The mortgage industry is a prime example of an industry that should have predicted the collapse. I knew there was a problem when my friend who worked in fast food and her boyfriend bought a $750,000 three-bedroom, middle-unit townhouse. There was no way they could afford that house. So many people ignored what was right in front of them and were caught off guard. Everyone was shocked when the obvious happened, and the housing prices tanked. It became a lot tougher to get a loan, and foreclosures were at their highest rates because all of those negative amortization, interest only, adjustable-rate mortgages were resetting.

Are you going to keep ignoring what's right in front of you, or are you going to learn from others' experience? Even if you personally did not experience the effects of the collapse, you likely know people who have. You can learn from their experiences too. Right before the collapse I remember my client selling their 850 square foot, two-bedroom house for $650,000 because they knew what others did not know; that it was time to get out.

Now let's take a look at a different industry, the U.S. car industry. How could they have not anticipated they would have to start getting serious about fuel efficiency and the economy? Now they are way behind the eight ball. Traditional media, the television, and newspaper industries are next. Most of the major media outlets will collapse. The few that will survive are operating their business from a state of Supreme Awareness. And thanks to Covid-19, the whole world is reshaping and resetting how we do everything right before our eyes. Social distancing required more businesses to move online, and one thing is definitely clear: If you cannot make money virtually, you will definitely get left behind.

One of the best things about being an entrepreneur is that if you can see what is happening around you and if you are aware of what is happening in the world on a spiritual level, you will have all the power and insight that you need. Your business is not like all of those other giant conglomerates that cannot course correct in time because they have to get buy-ins from a board of directors, lawyers, accountants, and investors before they are able to make decisions. You don't have all of these layers of accountability to hide behind. The only one responsible for your success is you. This is both a blessing and a curse. Whether it is your blessing, or your lesson will depend on whether you are operating your business from a place of Supreme Awareness or whether your eyes are closed in denial, blame, and fear. Are you willing to do the difficult things and make the difficult decisions? Are you willing to act from a place of right action, even when you are scared, or it's hard, or you simply don't feel like it?

Well it is time to wake up, open your eyes, and operate your business from a place of Supreme Awareness and treat your business like a real business. It is time to show up like you know you can. Do anything less, and you might as well get a job. Not only would it be easier and less stressful, but it will also be fairer to you and your family. Truth be told, if you don't treat your business like a business, it is simply going to be too much of a struggle to keep it going.

This does not mean that you have to build a big business and lose your soul in the process. The goal is to infuse your business with your soul by utilizing the laws of the universe (we'll get into that later in the book). And you don't have to work all the time. In fact, it is the exact opposite. Treat your business like a business, and you can eventually work part-time hours, work from home or anywhere else in the world, and build a tremendous fortune. So how do you treat your business like a true business? It starts by building a solid **Black Wall Street LIFT Foundation** by giving your business the **L**egal, **I**nsurance, **F**inance, and **T**ax systems needed to thrive. This is how you give your business the respect it needs to ensure it has a real deal, solid foundation underneath it. If you fail to do this, you will always be stressed out, wondering when something bad will happen or whether your business will make it for the long haul. This is no way to live your life. You started your business so you could have freedom, not constant stress and worry.

The good news is that it is never too late to do the right thing. No matter where you are in your business, whether you are just starting out, or recently hit six figures approaching seven, or have been in business for years, you can still build a wildly successful, Supremely Aware business.

Today, more and more people than ever before are leaving their jobs and entering the entrepreneurial world. Most of them have no idea how to build a real, rock-solid business, and maybe you don't either—until now. The good news for you is that you are at a huge advantage by simply reading this book. If you merely take one action or one idea you get from this book, you will be ahead of the game. If you implement two ideas, you will be way ahead of the game. And suppose you implement three or more recommendations? In that case, you will absolutely, positively, without a doubt be on track to not only find financial freedom, but also make a tremendous impact in the world. Most people do nothing. And maybe until now, you know you haven't been doing as much as you can from a "take your business serious" perspective. Maybe you know that your financial systems are shaky or that there are certain reports you know you should look at every month, but you don't. Maybe you have a few undocumented agreements floating around in the universe that could possibly come back to haunt you one day, or maybe they already have. Maybe you are in the midst of disputes and conflict with people important to you and your business, or even in your life which keeps you from focusing on making money and impacting the world. Maybe you suspect that you have tax problems and don't know where to begin.

I know one imaginary business owner who has not filed a tax return in two years because the company he hired to do it dropped the ball, and he did not follow up with them because he just didn't want to deal with it. On the one hand, no one wants to deal with Uncle Sam, so I get it. On the other hand, WTF!? This is one of those things that not only will come back to bite him in the future, but it will hold him back by keeping his business from truly thriving. Maybe you are not sure if you have the right insurance, or you don't have any insurance at all, and you know you really need to look into that. I could go on and on about the holes you may have in your business, but here's the bottom line: When you know you do not have a solid foundation, it is reflected in the way you show up in your business and the way you show up in the world. Your prospects will not take you seriously, your clients will have less trust in you, vendors will not fulfill your needs first, and investors won't come knocking on your door. Well, do investors ever really come knocking at your door? They might if you get serious about how you show up in the world. When you begin to take your business seriously, so will everyone else.

If you begin the process now, within six to nine months, you can have a business that has a solid **Black Wall Street LIFT Foundation** beneath it, so you can have unshakable confidence that your business will never let you or your family down. Once you have a solid **LIFT** foundation, you'll find yourself naturally leveraging your time, inspiring others, enjoying financial freedom, and living your truth out loud for the whole world to see. But before we dive into the laws of the land, we begin with the Alpha and Omega, the beginning and the end–that from which all power begins.

CHAPTER I

The Laws of The Universe

"You have to believe in gods to see them."
~ Hopi Indian Saying

You can do anything! And when I say anything, I mean you can do absolutely anything! Forgive me for sounding redundant, but I am still running on adrenaline from riding a bicycle from Houston, Texas, to New Orleans, Louisiana after only three and a half weeks of training. The total ride was 533 miles, and it may have been one of the most rewarding experiences of my entire life, second only to taking and passing the bar exam to become a licensed attorney 15 years ago. People called me crazy for attempting such a difficult feat since I am not a seasoned cyclist or even your typical athlete, but there is something I find exhilarating about achieving the impossible. It just really gets me going. I knew it was time to grow into my summer body, and growth doesn't happen in comfort zones. I learned a long time ago, no one truly knows what he/she can do until they do it, so why not give it a try?

"Fortune does favor the bold, and you'll never know what you are capable of if you don't try." ~ Sheryl Sandberg.

This habit of pushing myself beyond my limit began during my childhood. I grew up in Sunnyside—on the Southside of Houston, Texas. Back then, I was constantly told I was pretty, but not smart. The only reason I became an attorney in the first place was because my aunt told me it was impossible. The same aunt who bragged about her ability to receive a government check by telling doctors a talking pig was telling her to hurt people. She was a career criminal, which made her the family attorney by default because in the hood, no one knows the law better than a criminal. Take note: **Your greatest problem will always be your greatest opportunity.** I didn't know if I could become an attorney either; I had never done it before. In fact, no one in my family had done it before either. My desire to become an attorney grew out of my family telling me it was impossible. **Another problem turned into an opportunity yet again!**

You don't know how far you can go unless you push yourself beyond your comfort zone. I did more than push. I charged! I sat on the front row in all of my college courses and made it a point to do every assignment provided, including extra credit because, according to my family, I needed all the help I could get. I made the Dean's List multiple times at Sam Houston State University and received two Ameris Jurisprudence awards in law school for obtaining the highest grades in evidence and commercial paper. In the end, I learned I was quite brilliant. My only regret was not setting my goals higher.

I am a southern belle from Houston, Texas. I attended Sam Houston State University up the street in Huntsville, Texas, and Thurgood Marshall School of Law in downtown Houston. I didn't go anywhere. While I am grateful for my college career and the jewels I received from attending Thurgood Marshall School of Law at Texas Southern University, where I learned that *"A lawyer who is not a social engi-*

neer is a social parasite," I always wondered if I could have con-
quered Harvard or the bright lights of New York City, which leads me
to my next point.

Have you ever wondered why climbing success is compared to
climbing a ladder? The analogy works for several reasons. One is that
a ladder must be climbed one rung at a time, just as success happens
step-by-step. People do not explode into success; they grow into success, so remember to be patient with yourself along the way. There
was no way I could see Harvard from Sunnyside, Houston, Texas. In
2013, the Houston Chronicle reported Sunnyside as the sixth most
dangerous neighborhood in America. According to statistics, I was
supposed to get pregnant, drop out of high school, and raise my baby
in a crack house. According to the data, I was lucky.

Thanks to several mentors, including Texas State Senator turned
Harris County Commissioner, Rodney Ellis; Texas State Representative Dr. Alma A. Allen; and the Black Bull of Wall Street, I was able
to see that I had within me all the power that I needed to achieve all
that I desired in life. To date, I am the first and only attorney in my
family. I also have the highest level of education in my family, holding a Juris Doctorate in law, licensed to practice law in the great states
of Texas and New York. Actually, I have an older cousin who recently received her Ph.D.– congrats cousin! Climbing the ladder rung by
rung, the little girl from the Southside of Houston, Texas, became
TheWallStreetLawyer.com.

Remember the family member who told me I could never become
an attorney? The one with the talking pig who received a government
check? Well when I moved on Wall Street, there was a huge pig parade there to welcome me! And I do mean this literally; I can't make

this stuff up. Marching through the financial capital of the world I watched a parade go by with a marching band big enough to rival Beyonce's BeyChella Marching Band. The band members were dressed in pink from head to toe, with pig emblems on the front of their uniforms. They marched down Broad Street right in front of the New York Stock Exchange, holding a string to a giant pig floating in the air. Giant pig balloons were everywhere, and there was pig jerky all over the place. The giant marching sign read: *Super Pig, a clear cut above all other porks!*

I later found out they were filming a big-budget film called *Okja* about a super pig. If you are interested in watching the movie, you should check it out on Netflix. I sure did. It was awesome to see God's work come full circle in my life. Because my aunt, the one who told me I would never be an attorney, the one who received a government check thanks to her imaginary talking pig, is also the same person who inspired me to become a lawyer. And not only did I become a lawyer, I became TheWallStreetLawyer.com. And the day that I moved on Wall Street there was a whole pig parade in the financial capital of the world, with hundreds of people dressed in pig costumes there to welcome me! And it was absolutely perfect. So perfect it looked like it was planned to happen this way before the beginning of time, before I was even thought of. God sure does have a funny sense of humor. I guess problems really are opportunities in disguise, and pigs really do fly.

You see, the universe accomplishes everything with zero effort. The grass doesn't strain to grow. It grows effortlessly. It is just this great design created by The Great I AM, with everything flowing and operating in perfect harmony. Understanding the laws of the universe will help you master your life on all levels and give you insight into what you need to do to reach your goals. As an attorney, business, and manifestation coach, the universal law of attraction is a key component to the work that I do with my clients to help them build a fulfilling life and business that they truly desire and love. However, the law of attraction is only one piece of a big puzzle and only one of many laws you need to help you design the life of your dreams.

There are actually 12 universal laws people speak about that play out in our lives, and the one that I am adding to the list, the 13th law. So I believe there are 13 laws that will help you master your life on all levels and give you insight into what you can do to reach your goals from a heavenly holistic perspective.

THE LAW OF DIVINE ONENESS

The first and foundational law of the universe is called the law of divine oneness, which highlights the interconnectedness of all things. Another way of stating it is that we are all connected through the law of creation. We are all one. And because we are all one, everything that we do will have a ripple effect and impact on the collective universe, not just our own individual lives. The thing to remember here is that your actions both matter and make a difference. Think about the impact that a little pebble has when you throw it into a body of water, like the ocean, and you see one ripple, and another ripple, and then another. Think about each wave and how each wave builds upon and influences the next wave. To work with the law of oneness, one must ask questions like, "How can I make a difference? How can I show more compassion and acceptance for those I do not understand? What would love do?"

THE LAW OF VIBRATION

The second law is the law of vibration. One of the greatest discoveries of all ages is that of physical science, which shows that all things have their source and being in vibration. What this means is that according to the law of vibration, everything is constantly moving and constantly carrying energy. This applies to enormous parts of the universe like planets and stars, but it also applies to smaller parts of the universe like this book that you are reading right now. It follows from this truth that everything has its own specific energy frequency, and items of similar vibration are attracted to each other. In other words, birds of a feather flock together. To use this law to manifest your desires, you must match the vibration of that which you want to manifest or attract to you. Higher energies are attracted to higher energies, and lower vibration energies tend to attract lower vibration energies. This is why someone who receives a large amount of money may not be able to hold onto it, like someone who wins the lottery for example. Most people think, *how can someone win that much money and not be able to hold on to it?* The answer is simple. That person has a low vibration when it comes to money. That person will always have a low vibration when it comes to money, which will manifest in them not having money in the physical reality unless they do something to raise their financial vibration. If you feel the need to elevate your financial vibration and increase your "good vibes for success," there are many great practices and tools that will help you do so, like yoga, sunbathing and chakra work. You should also check out some of the resources **we have at our resource center at Black-WallStreet.com**.

THE LAW OF CORRESPONDENCE
As Above So Below, As Within So Without

The third law of the universe is the law of correspondence, which states that the reality around us is a mirror of what's happening inside of us at any given moment in time. This law is directly related to the foundational law of the law of divine oneness of everything being interconnected. The key here is to look for patterns in your own life and in your way of thinking and notice how these patterns repeat for you and repeat elsewhere in the world. Because the premise behind the law of correspondence is that our lives are created by the subconscious patterns present every single day, and these patterns either serve us or they hold us back.

You activate this law in your life by becoming aware of your own patterns, which are often passed down to you from family ties, and even the media through marketing. Once recognized, you can then consciously take action steps to disrupt or break them. Remember, generational curses stop when you stop them. And you have everything you need inside of you to overcome conditioned thinking.

THE LAW OF ATTRACTION

Unquestionably the most popular and talked about universal law on the list, the fourth law, is the law of attraction, which is also known as the law of vibration in action. This law is popular because it is what people focus on most to help them master the art of manifestation. It gained national attention in a book and documentary endorsed by Oprah, called *The Secret*. The law of attraction states that like attracts like, which is another way of saying that you draw to yourself that which you are. It is realizing that you are the co-creator of your life *along with* God. As magnetic beings, our souls work perfectly within the law of attraction and draw to us exactly what we create with our thoughts. What you think has a tremendous influence on how your soul will experience life. The Law of Attraction is the science behind how prayer works, and it explains the why behind when the praises go up, the blessings rain down. It's all about matching energies and vibrations on a subconscious energetic level. In order to change your life on the physical plane, one must change themselves subconsciously first, then watch in awe as the universe responds and matches that inner feeling. It follows that if you want to have more love in your life, you have to be more loving. If you want to have more success in your life, you have to become more successful energetically. This law is a very clear mirror of your self-worth and the mindset which you carry because you are constantly surrounded by the outcome of the decisions, thoughts, and actions that you made in the past. The beautiful thing about this law is that on any given day, you are fully capable of making other decisions and attracting a whole new set of circumstances to experience in the future. I guarantee you right now, if you are consciously reading this book, consciously seeking out these laws and improving your life, your reality will reflect that. Just make sure you write it down to help you analyze the synchronicities and chart your growth in your **Black Wall Street Business Journal**. Because the more miracles you acknowledge, the more miracles will appear.

In order to have the things you desire in your life, you have to figure out how to get your energy to vibrate in the same frequency as the things you wish to attract. It is written that by being positive, proactive, and loving (because we are all vibrational beings) by the law of attraction, you will attract more of the same into your life. Meanwhile, pessimism, fear, and being lethargic will lead you to generate more negative experiences and other low vibration experiences in your life. By working to create a more positive life in your personal life and in your business, you are already using the law of attraction to create a better reality. If you would like more information on how to master the law of attraction in your business, **visit Black-WallStreet.com**.

THE LAW OF INSPIRED ACTION

The fifth law of the universe is the law of inspired action, which is closely related to and builds upon the previous law, the law of attraction. While the law of attraction is about vibrationally aligning yourself with what you want to attract or manifest in your life, the law of inspired action is about **taking those real, actionable steps to create** what you want in your life. I like to refer to this law as "the blind walk of faith." In my mind, this might be one of the most important laws because this is where all of the other laws sort of come together. As human beings with limited perceptions, we do not know "how" God will provide a way. The "how" is revealed one step, one rung at a time. You activate the law of inspired action by following the urge and inspiration to, well you guessed it, take the next step! And when you take that step, another step will appear as if by magic–like a car that is traveling through the night with the lights on. Even though it can only see what is right in front of it, it can make it all the way from Texas to New York because you only need to see the next step. And as long as you can see the next step, each step will eventually lead you to where it is that you want to be.

How do you know if the next step is actually the next right action? Have you ever had that idea that you knew was so right, and everyone else around you thought was crazy? When you have inspired action, you and your path will light up like a Christmas tree. You will be so inspired, so turned on, that you will basically run into action unbridled by fear. To activate this law, you must first get inspired, then take action from that place of alignment. It's about knowing when divine inspiration strikes, then acting on that inspiration quickly. When people talk about creativity, they are actually talking about this inspired action in motion. This is a little bit different from being motivated. Being motivated is ego-driven. It is you being motivated to do something. But when you are inspired, you are being moved to act from a subconscious level, moved by God, so to speak. It would behoove you to understand the difference. Because anytime you bring Infinite Intelligence, God, into the equation, that is when things will light up for you. That is where Supreme Love is. That is where things are moving at a very high frequency. Follow what keeps you at a high-frequency vibration, follow what brings you the most joy, and follow your bliss. That is where your answers lie. Become childlike in your pursuit of happiness and learn to live in hope, wonder, and excitement. This is the energy you are looking for, and when you don't have this energy, you should withdraw, meditate, seek, and find. Do some yoga, exercise, and surrender–just let your mind wander. Get your ego into the space where you can let go because when you let go of your need to control how things will work out, God can work things out, enter your awareness, and inspire you again. Because you are now again open to all of life's possibilities and to new ways of achieving your goals that you probably would never have thought of on your own. This is why you have to clear your mind and become a gateway for that inspiration. Because I can tell you this, if you've never made a million dollars before, you sure don't know how you are going to do that. But again, the "how" is not your business; the "how" is up to God, Infinite Intelligence, and that "how" will be revealed to you as long as you believe in and are committed to the dream, doing the work to raise your vibration, and maintaining the faith of a child.

THE LAW OF PERPETUAL
TRANSMUTATION OF ENERGY

The sixth law is the law of perpetual transmutation of energy. I know I said the last law was the most important law, but this one is my favorite. I really like this law because I've mastered the art of transmutation, transmuting negative energy and negative experiences into opportunities and rewards for myself. And this is something I love to talk about and will explore in further detail in the 13th law, but I digress. The law of perpetual transmutation of energy states that energy is always constantly evolving, moving in and out of form and that everything is constantly in a state of flux. This law is so important because it brings into our awareness how we can trigger positive changes in our own lives, keeping in mind that high vibrations trigger improvements in low vibrations. Let me repeat this. High vibration activities will improve the vibration of low frequencies. This means that if you are vibrating at a low frequency, exposing yourself to high frequency–happy, encouraging, uplifting, and upbeat people, places, and things will naturally trigger that brighter transmutation of the negative energy that is within you. This law means that even the smallest actions can have the most profound effect, no different from the seed of a mighty tree holding all of its promise in its tiny shell– you also have the power within you to move mountains. So how do you put this law into action on a practical level? Remember, higher frequencies transmute lower vibrations into high energy when applied with intention.

To master this law on a practical level, you should actively seek to uplift negative energy around you by making changes to your environment. Do small things every day to uplift your energy. Whether that is dancing like no one is watching and singing like no one is listening, these small shifts will equal major results in your life and in your business. Every time you work on your corporate foundation by setting up your Legal, Insurance, Finance, and Tax systems for success, you are doing high-vibration activities to shore up your success. Every little thing that you do to nurture your business is bringing you new business. A baby business has so much promise–like that seed with the promise of becoming the mighty oak tree, you too carry all of that promise. And every time you till the soil, you are nurturing your business towards success.

THE LAW OF CAUSE AND EFFECT

The seventh law, the law of cause and effect, directly flows from that perpetual transmutation of energy in that there is a direct relation between the actions you take and your results. Also known as the law of karma, it has been said that everything you put out into the universe always comes back to you threefold. To harness this power, be aware of how your actions and decisions affect not just you but everyone else around you. Focus on sending out good vibes only because if you are coming from a place of anger or resentment, and you put that energy out there, you will eventually be affected as a result by having this same energy come back to you. It is very interesting how all of these laws tie into one another because this is the law of attraction and the law of vibration in action. I like to think of it like this: We are really just looking at universal truths from all angles to understand how we as human beings create our reality.

THE LAW OF COMPENSATION

The eighth law is the law of compensation. The law of compensation relates closer to the law of attraction and law of correspondence in that you reap what you sow. It instills trust in us that we will be compensated for our work in the world, as long as we are open to receiving it in all the many ways the world can deliver. The key is to be open to receiving compensation in *all* forms–including love, joy, kindness, and respect, in addition to financial gain. Everything you do, everything you put out into the world, every seed you plant will be rewarded threefold. The way to work with this law is to ask yourself, "Where am I being called to serve mankind? Where am I being called to serve my community? How am I being called to serve and support the world today?" This law is a breeding ground for opportunity and self-discovery and also reminds me of the movie *Avatar*. I love this movie. I especially loved seeing the indigenous blue people who were fighting with bows and arrows (and the power of the universe) defeat the highly sophisticated army equipped with advanced technology beyond their native comprehension. Take note, when you are doing something for the good of your community and mankind as a whole, the universe will jump in and help you. This is how the natives defeated the sophisticated army and sent them back to their concrete world. Even the animals came in and were on cue to defend their sacred habitat. This is what comes to my mind when I think about the law of compensation. Service is actually one of my secret ingredients for massive success. The more people you serve, the more money you will make. So my gift to you, InTheBlackResources.com, online business, building resources to help keep you and your bank account in the black, is really a gift to myself. Zig Ziglar said it best: *"You can*

have everything in life you want if you will just help other people get
what they want."

THE LAW OF RELATIVITY

The ninth law is the law of relativity. The law of relativity directly relates to the law that I coined in law 13, which is the law of adversity. The law of relativity states that everything is relative. In reality,
everything is not good or bad but neutral because there is more than
one perspective on any situation and challenge. In the end, meaning
comes down to our particular perspective and perception. In other
words, it is your perception that will determine and create your reality, even more so than the reality itself. Applying this law will help
you understand the rougher parts of your life with greater compassion.
For example, if you are feeling ungrateful or feeling sorry for yourself, it is probably because you are comparing yourself to someone
else. If you stop comparing yourself to someone else, maybe you
could be more appreciative of what you do have. Mastery of this law
is how I discovered law 13, the law of adversity. But more on that later. To work with this law you must remain conscious of the fact that
there are always multiple perspectives on everything that happens to
you in your life. It is we who are the ones who assign meaning to
things. We have the power to consciously regard something as good
or bad regardless of outward appearances. Master this, and you will
always remain in your power.

THE LAW OF POLARITY

The tenth law is the law of polarity. Under the law of polarity,
everything has a polar opposite where one cannot exist without the

other. Up/down, light/dark, good/evil, and love/fear. There are always two sides to every coin. Experiencing these polarities is par for par and part of the human experience. Polarity helps us to learn from our mistakes by supporting us and identifying what we do not want so that we can become clearer on **what it is that we do want.** The mantra for this law is: Contrast brings more clarity. For example, if you are facing a health challenge or a challenge in the love department, tune into what the opposite looks like, and that will reveal a new perspective or lesson that you may need to learn.

THE LAW OF PERPETUAL MOTION (THE LAW OF RHYTHM)

The 11th law, the law of rhythm, is also known as the law of perpetual motion. This law is unsurprisingly focused on movement, which appeals to my inner drummer. In particular, the law of rhythm refers to the fact that all things come in cycles. We see this law express itself in nature with the seasons and in the body's aging process and life stages. Reflecting on this will help you gain perspective about your particular reality. For instance, the cycles of life have you starting from a newborn until about preteen. Then you have your teenage years, your twenties, your thirties, your forties, and so on. In each of these cycles, you start at the beginning of something, and then you ascend to a new level, then you master it, and then you start back over again at the beginning. We see those cycles in the human phases, just like we see the natural cycle of a tree being born, dying, and then pollinating to be reborn again. I know we don't talk about trees as being reborn, but you get the idea. The mantra meditation that comes to my mind for the law of rhythm or the law of perpetual motion is, "This too shall pass," from James Allen's *As a Man Thinketh.*

THE LAW OF GIVING AND RECEIVING
(THE LAW OF GENDER)

The 12th law of the universe is the law of gender, which is also known as the law of giving and receiving. The law of gender really has very little to do with biological gender and actually refers to the fact that two major types of energy exist in the world—the polarity between masculine and feminine energy, yin and the yang, and light and dark. Every human being has both masculine and feminine energy. The goal is to find a way to achieve balance between these two polarities in order to live an authentic and happy life. The masculine energy is referred to as the ego, which is your outward manifestation. The feminine energy is referred to as your subconscious and your inner world, the world guided by your intuition. Maybe she's born with it. Maybe it's women's intuition, LOL. If you are a black woman, you have added soul power when you consider what melanin does for creativity. Did you know melanin is produced in the pineal gland, the same part of the brain that is referred to as the seat of the soul? It then follows that *having soul* goes far beyond James Brown and the dance floor. It transcends the universe.

"Say it loud, I'm Black and I'm PROUD!"
~ James Brown

To work with this law, make sure that your masculine energy and feminine energy are in harmony with one another and that you are giving and receiving in equal measure. To work with this law in your business is to recognize where your giving and receiving may be off base and to figure out what it is that you can do to make sure they are in harmony with one another, which will definitely affect your financial bottom line.

THE LAW OF ADVERSITY

"The Shamans say that being a medicine man begins by falling into the power of the demons. The one who pulls out of the dark place be-comes the medicine man, and the one who stays in it is the sick per-son. You can take every psychological illness as an initiation. Even the worst things you fall into are an initiation, for you are in some-thing which belongs to you."
~ Joan Halifax

Last but not least, the 13th law, the law that I coined, is the law of adversity. It has been said frequently that the Chinese word for crisis is composed of two Chinese characters signifying danger and oppor-tunity. According to Wikipedia, the phrase became popular when JFK used it in his campaign speeches in 1959 and 1960. Referring to the word has since become a staple example for American business con-sultants and motivational speakers worldwide. Even though it is a misinterpretation, I don't see any reason to change it now. :-)

Every single problem is an opportunity in disguise. Mastering the law of adversity, I have built my entire life and career using what the world discarded. I became the alchemist in my own life by transmut-ing trauma and the energy of the problem into an opportunity for my-self. I have been able to do this by changing my perspective about the problem altogether. To begin with, I believe wholeheartedly that God loves me unconditionally. Following that, I believe God loves me too much to allow me to suffer the darkness of this world in vain. If he is allowing darkness, stress, and strain to rain into my reality, it has to be for a good reason. I understand that the rain clouds in my life also bring life's sustenance. In my suffering I drink well, and I grow strong.

Today I am so advanced that when the shit hits the fan, I immediately go into praise mode and begin searching for the opportunity within the problem to help me pass through the adversity a lot quicker. This is my secret bullish, sacred survival technique. Use it wisely. To activate this law in the valley one need only remember, "Life is not happening to me. Life is happening for me."

Mature beings who understand all of the other 12 laws are able to pass through adversity with clarity, the kind of clarity that allows them to see the rainbow that leads to the pot of gold. It is guaranteed. I like to take it a step further and say that the opportunity presented through the adversity, by law, shows up in equal measure. In other words, if the problem is extremely hard, the blessing will be just as, if not ten times more, amazing. The reward is always equal or better–two sides of the same coin. Understanding these universal truths is like wearing a pair of magic glasses, which gives you perspective and vision. And vision is extremely important because everybody gets lemons. Lemons alone will not give you lemonade. You have to *see* the lemonade that can be made from the lemons before you know what work needs to be done. Then you have to put in the work. But if you do the work presented to you in these 13 laws of the universe and the foundational work found in the remainder of this book, your hard work will definitely pay you dividends long into the future. It will feel like a spiritual jetpack of universal love elevating you toward higher ground. Dedicate each step you take toward keeping your eyes on the prize, becoming more awake and aware, knowing that as you are lifted, we all are lifted.

Rise in Black Power.

CHAPTER II

Analogy

Having coached many entrepreneurs to financial success throughout my career, one thing I've learned is that everyone has different learning styles. Generally, people fall into two categories. They are either artists or engineers. The artists among you are right-brain visual learners. The engineers are left-brain logical learners. By integrating both learning styles, I am able to drive the messages in this book home more powerfully. My goal is to not only inform you but to transform you into an enlightened, spiritual entrepreneur. Transformation is a thorough or dramatic change in form or appearance, a metamorphosis during the life cycle of an animal. What is a metamorphosis? A metamorphosis is a change of the form or nature of a thing or person into a completely different one by natural or supernatural means.

Consider the transformation in the following, *Who needs a boat?*

Who Needs a Boat?

Chapter One. I wake up hungry. I decide to fish. I take out the boat and toss over my net. A storm comes and swallows my boat. I almost drown. It is not my fault.

Chapter Two. I wake up to fish for food. I take out my boat and toss over my net. A storm comes. It's bumpy, but I survive. The fish I catch do not. My food is lost at sea. It is not my fault.

Chapter Three. I wake up to fish for food. I take the boat out and toss over my net to catch fish. A storm comes. It's bumpy, but I survive. The fish I catch do not. My food is lost at sea. It is my fault. My eyes are open. I will do better next time.

Chapter Four. I wake up early to fish for food. I take out the boat and toss over my net. A storm comes. It was exciting! It was bumpy, but I managed to survive, and so does my catch!

I think I saw God.

Chapter Five. I wake up, and I thank God for today's daily bread. I walk outside, and I notice the storm washed an abundance of fish upon my shore.

All Praises To The Most High.

CHAPTER III

The Laws of The Land

"Laws grind the poor, and rich men rule the law."
~ Oliver Goldsmith, *The Traveller*

LIFT Overview

The law of the land is the whole body of valid laws, statutory or otherwise, existing and in force in a country or jurisdiction at any given time. The term was used in 1787 to write the supremacy clause of the United States Constitution, which established that the federal constitution and federal law generally take precedence over state laws and state constitutions. In other words, the Constitution of the United States of America shall be the supreme law of the land.

The supremacy clause is the only place in the constitution where this exact term was used. If you think of the United States Constitution as the supreme law of the land, consider our **LIFT** systems that you are about to learn in this book as the supreme laws in business because that is exactly what it is. By definition, the law is a system of rules that a particular country or community recognizes as regulating the actions of its members and which it may enforce by the imposition of penalties. When we speak about the laws that you need to organize, sustain, and grow a sellable million-dollar business, we're talking about systems that you need to have in place to prime you, and your business for success. The way that we teach these systems is what we refer to on Black Wall Street as **LIFT** - **L**egal, **I**nsurance, **F**inance, and **T**ax. Foundational systems that every business needs in place to **LIFT** that business up to the stratosphere of success and beyond. Our **Black Wall Street LIFT Foundation Systems** will ensure that your business is positioned for exponential growth by addressing four often overlooked areas (**L**egal, **I**nsurance, **F**inance, and **T**ax). As you learn about our **LIFT** systems explained throughout this book, consider where the holes might be in your own **LIFT** foundation so that you know exactly what you need to do to get and keep your business **In The Black.**

Once you complete this book and our accompanying course, you will know without a shadow of a doubt that your business is built on the rock-solid foundation needed to support and leverage your time, inspire others, enjoy financial freedom, and live your truth out loud for the world to see! You will learn exactly who you need on your team and what you can do by yourself. Having a solid **Black Wall Street LIFT Foundation** in your business can be the difference between building a business built of straw and hay that can be blown down as soon as life's obstacles and situations arise, and a real business built of bricks that can withstand the test of time and do real business in the world. It doesn't matter if you are Mark Zuckerberg or Beyonce; every business needs these four systems in place so that it has the necessary foundation to succeed. Think about it this way, A shark in a fish tank would grow eight inches, but in the ocean, it would grow to eight feet or more. The shark will never outgrow its environment, and neither will you.

Many times in business we play small-minded, and our business-es do not have the nutrition and sustenance they need to grow. Change the environment of your business and watch it grow to infinity and beyond. Remember, your business can only grow as successfully, as impactfully, and financially fulfilling as your **LIFT** foundations will allow. As I mentioned earlier, our **Black Wall Street LIFT Foundation** is the **L**egal, **I**nsurance, **F**inance, and **T**ax systems that every business must have in place. Most business owners are losing out on tremendous growth opportunities because they simply do not want to pay attention to these important items on their very important things to-do list. They don't see them as revenue-generating, client-attracting, or business-building, so they are often ignored. Because of this, the business falls short. When your business is not built on a sol-id, firm foundation, your business is built like a house of straw. You are only one challenge, one roadblock, or one obstacle from being blown away.

You should also consider that in today's age of information and awareness, your prospects and customers can sense when your busi-ness is not built on a solid foundation. Your customers will know not to take you as seriously as the next business, and that could really af-fect your bottom line. Investors and lenders, banks, and people with money won't even look at you. And worst of all, you will know you aren't really taking your business seriously, which will affect the way you show up in the world. Let's be clear. Any real business that is making an impact in the world has a solid **LIFT** foundation in place, whether or not they call it this. It is what every business *needs* to grow and build a meaningful, sustainable, impactful business for the long term. It will allow you to create a legacy for you and your family that you can pass down from generation to generation, which means it is also the foundation to creating black generational wealth.

So let's just get into it. The first initial in our **Black Wall Street LIFT Foundation** stands for the **Legal Pillar**. We start with the legal entity of your business. We always start with the legal entity of your business, and the first question we ask is: Do you really need to have a business entity in place? Many people believe that they do not need a business entity in place. They believe they can just start doing business, give themselves a name, maybe get a DBA (doing business as) certificate filed with their local county, and boom! They are in business. So, do you actually *need* a business entity? What are the benefits of having one?

There are many reasons why you need a business entity, but the main reason is to protect your personal assets from the activities of your business. Once you set up a business entity, personal assets like your home, personal bank accounts, your retirement accounts, and everything that you are building for you and your family will be protected from the activities of your business. Why do you want to keep your personal assets separate from your business? It's simple. In business and in life, where there is no risk, there is no reward. If you are building a business that is going to be a big business that will have a big impact on the world, you will have to take some big risks. It's the only way to grow. Whenever you are taking these risks to grow your business, you don't want to put your personal assets at risk. You create a business entity to create a shield of protection between your business activities and your personal assets.

What do some of these risks look like? They look like employees and independent contractors and the money you put into the business to grow it. You have leases that you enter into, corporate agreements, and you may or may not drive a car in the name of your business. If you are interacting in the world through your business and don't have a business entity in place, you are personally on the hook if anything goes wrong. So why not set up a business entity? This is America – good, bad, or indifferent, and this country was built on capitalism. That being said, those who move in the spirit of capitalism and capitalize on the opportunities presented stand to win and many times achieve the American dream despite the color of their skin.

"I too am America." ~ Langston Hughes

Now I know what you are thinking, "I already have my business entity set up, so I'm good to go. There is nothing else I need to worry about." Unfortunately, that is not the truth, and there are many lawyers and law firms today who give advice this way.

They start up the LLC/INC, crank out an operating agreement or a shareholders agreement if the client has a corporation, and tuck those papers away in a cabinet and go on about their business. This is not enough. Most lawyers have been trained on an old, outdated business model that goes a little something like this:

- You go to the lawyer's office after you've had a consultation.

- The lawyer recommends a specific type of business entity, probably an LLC or an S-Corp, charges a flat fee to set it up, and prepares a document for you to sign.

- You take your documents home, and you put them away in your corporate record book up on the shelf.

- You look at the book. You see it. Maybe you got a fancy corporate book from a CPA, or you ordered it yourself because you set up your own business online through a business startup service.

No matter how you set that business up, it is probably not enough and might not be done right because you probably never talked to your attorney again. For most business owners, from the moment the paperwork is filed away, they are off to doing business as usual. What they do not realize, and what most attorneys fail to tell you, is that in order for your business entity to really protect your assets, you have to **maintain that business entity over time**. It means that you need to have corporate resolutions where you take notes about what your business is doing forever and ever, amen. For example, if you buy insurance, you hire someone, or you borrow money, all of that should be documented in your corporate resolutions, which you keep a record of in your corporate record book. In addition, every year you must keep your meeting minutes up to date. This means that you should have an **annual meeting**, and you should keep a record of this on an ongoing basis. You should have a record of the stock certificates or membership interests that your company has issued. What is a stock certificate? A **stock certificate**, or **member certificate** if you have an LLC, shows you who owns the company. You may have them sitting in your corporate record book, but if you are like most people, you probably never filled them out and issued them to the owners of the company.

It is the setup of your business and the ongoing tracking of your corporate business records that really allow you to maintain that shield of protection over time. What happens when you don't have these records in your business? If you do not have these records set up when something happens in your business, like being threatened or served with a lawsuit or being audited, you will be scrambling to gather all of this information at the last minute. When it is time to pay your taxes, you will be scrambling at the last minute in your financial systems and tax systems to bring your business up to code to get the filing done. Trust me. It will save you a lot of headache, time, and money. It's a lot easier if you are maintaining your business and documenting your business throughout the entire year.

I am an optimist. You will always hear me speak about using mind over matter to obtain more matter in the world in which we live. And even though I'm a lawyer, I don't like to think about things like lawsuits and audits, etc., but these are not things to be afraid of. These are the simple realities of doing business. A reality that no one likes to talk about, but it is a reality that you can and must be prepared for, nonetheless. Disagreements and disputes are part of doing business. They are nothing to be afraid of, especially when you have business systems in place to give your business the strength and foundation it needs to succeed. When you are properly prepared, and you've built a solid foundation, a business built with bricks and not straw like the three little piggies, you have a business that you don't have to worry about. When conflicts, disagreements, and disputes arise, you will be able to deal with them directly, straight forward, and head-on and they will not take you from your normal course of business. This will allow you to do the things you do best in your business and make more money. Being prepared does not simply mean having a business entity in place. It means having the tools and systems to deal with the conflict that may arise without fear. It means having a business that has maintained its business status over time so that when conflicts and disputes do arise, you will be able to handle them easily and efficiently.

Look at it like this. We are all traveling down the same road in life. It is equipped with potholes, bumps in the roads, weird tricks, plot twists, and turns. How we prepare for and then handle all of these obstacles determines the degree of ease and harmony in our lives. The better prepared we are, the easier life is going to be.

Action Step:

Begin to ask your friends and family members if they have ever been sued or threatened with a lawsuit or if they have ever dealt with an audit in their business. You might be surprised at how many people you hear say, "Yes." This will help you overcome the negative connotation that lawsuits only happen to bad people, which is simply not true. Lawsuits happen to people who are doing business and moving throughout the world. The facts of the lawsuit determine the character of the people–remember that. If you are in business, at some point you will be threatened with a lawsuit and/or sued. If not, it might mean you are not putting yourself out in the world in a big enough way. When you are playing a really big game and putting yourself out there in a really big way, it is a reality of human nature that people who want to pull you down will be drawn to you. They feel entitled, and they want to take what they feel that they are entitled to. Having your legal structures in place will allow you to deal with these threats without worry, doubt, or fear. If you have not set up everything the right way, like having your corporate resolutions, meeting minutes, stock certificates, and everything else you really need to have for your business set up, you leave yourself threatened and exposed because the business entity will not protect you from business risks. In fact, it is what we call *piercing the corporate veil*, which means the court will treat your business entity like it doesn't even exist (Yikes!).

LIFT Overview (contd.)

Remember, having the business entity set up is just the first step. Beyond having your business entity formed, you must also have documented agreements, meeting minutes, and corporate resolutions to document everything that the business is doing over time. You want to have that for your record-keeping, and you also want to have that to minimize the threats of lawsuits that could happen due to not having these things in place. **Undocumented oral agreements almost always guarantee a dispute further down the road.** Even if all of the people involved are good people with good intentions. Why? Because without an actual agreement in place, you have no way of knowing if you two are on the same page and in agreement with the same terms. We are all human beings, and we are always looking at things from our own human perspective. Such is life. Perspective is subjective and always open to interpretation. It's a variable based on where you are individually and how you see the world. Two different people under the same circumstances, same temperature, same room, using the same ingredients for their cakes, will come out with two completely different cakes, two completely different scenarios, and two completely different understandings. As a result, conflicts, disputes, and disagreements arise, all of which can become extremely time-consuming and expensive. It is your job and responsibility to anticipate them in advance and to document the process of your understanding in writing.

This is also a great place to incorporate some of your law of attraction and thinking things into existence teachings because this agreement is actually a great opportunity to shape the sort of relationship you want to have with your potential business partner, vendor, or employee. How someone is showing up for you in the documentation process is a wonderful indicator of how you two will be working together in the future for the long term. If you cannot get through the agreement/documentation process, be grateful. Chances are you wouldn't be able to do business with them anyway, and you may have just saved yourself a huge amount of time, heartache, and pain. At BlackWallStreet.com we set up simple steps to help guide you through the agreement documentation process. These steps will allow you to create agreements without getting a lawyer involved until it is absolutely necessary, saving yourself quite a bit of time and money on legal fees. Most importantly, you will have insight into whether or not the person you are working with is the type of person that you can work with long term. Again, I will walk you through the simple steps of creating your own legal agreements later in this book and in our companion course.

How do I know this? Everything I am laying out in this book is from my personal experiences and the experiences of my clients throughout the years. Did you know that every single independent contractor that you hire to do work for your business owns the product that they are creating outright without an express agreement giving it over to you? That means that if you are a musician and you hire someone to do a beat, or if you hire a business company or someone to build you a website, that company or person owns the website because they are an independent contractor and/or a separate business, and not an employee who works for you. That company owns the product of their intellectual property and their creations unless they have an agreement with you that says otherwise. There is a lot to cover in legal, and we'll do a deep dive later on in this book with action items and then a deeper dive with examples and "how-to" instructions in the course.

So for now, let's move on to the **Insurance Pillar**. Why do you need to have insurance? Having insurance offers you financial security and peace of mind to know that you are secured against any unforeseen events in life. All of us wish to achieve financial freedom at some point in our lives, and when it comes to doing that, we tend to believe that savings are enough to be financially stable. Savings and a thriving business. If you look at life from a practical perspective, you will understand that savings and a business alone are not enough to achieve financial freedom. Insuring your assets and your business with insurance policies is equally important. Many people believe that they do not need insurance policies because they can save enough money to replace their assets should anything happen to them. But consider a situation where you have to wipe out all of your assets to pay for medical bills, or a lawsuit arises because your business is being sued.

Let me give you a real-life example that happened to one of my clients. My client worked in the sales department for a major corporation for years. He and one of his business partners decided to leave the company they worked for and start their own competing company. The company they worked for sued them. Had they not had insurance in place, they would have been out of business within months because they would not have been able to pay for their legal defense themselves. They simply did not have enough cash on hand to do that. Fortunately for them, they had the right kind of insurance. The lawsuit went on for three years against their former employer, racking up $2 million in legal fees. Guess what? They won. Today, the company they started is a successful competitor earning millions of dollars a year on its own. They would have been out of business within months without the right type of insurance. Unfortunately for a different client of mine, they did not have the right type of insurance in place when they were sued. They were sued by a former employee because they didn't have their employment policies and procedures set up correctly. When they fired this employee, they did everything wrong, even though they thought they were doing everything right and were justified in firing that employee.

Nevertheless, the employee sued them, and they didn't have the right type of insurance in place. They were able to scrape up $10,000 out of their own pockets to hire an attorney to defend the lawsuit, but that was just for their initial retainer. Ultimately, they settled the lawsuit for a mid-five-figure settlement just because they could not continue to pay the legal fees to defend their case. This would not have happened if they had the right insurance in place. They had insurance, but why didn't they have the right insurance? They didn't have the right insurance in place because they went through an insurance person who was simply a salesman, a person who only takes orders, and not a true insurance advisor who could advise them on the right type of insurance they needed for the type of business that they actually had. Their insurance salesperson did not know anything about their business, so they could not recommend the right type of insurance products to protect them.

On the other hand, you also want to be wary of the insurance salesman who oversells the products and sells you things you don't need. The key to buying the right type of insurance for your businesses is to know exactly what you need and exactly what you do not need before you even contact an insurance advisor. In the insurance section of this book, and in our companion course, we give you everything that you need to make the right decisions about insurance coverage for you and your business.

Now, my favorite pillar, the **Finance Pillar.** This pillar covers the financial systems you need to have in place to ensure your business is financially successful. Let me be clear. The goal of every business is to make money. Despite this goal, this pillar seems to be the area where most business owners tend to make the most mistakes, myself included. Most business owners are managing their financial systems like this. They look at the bank account and see how much money is in the bank and spend whatever is there. This is no way to run a business. If you have had a little bit of training, you probably have a bookkeeper and are looking at your reports on a monthly basis. If you are like most small business owners, you glance at the reports, note what your incoming expenses are and how much money you have, whether you had a profit or a loss, and then you sit the report to the side. Here is the secret language of financial systems: When you understand what the secret language of your financial systems are saying, it's like having a crystal ball. You can predict and see into the future by knowing what your numbers are supposed to do, then predicting what they will continue to do, like clockwork, and having them show up that way, right on time, monthly, quarterly, and annually. Numbers are the key to every successful business, and as the saying goes, *Numbers don't lie.* In the finance pillar I will be showing you the exact reports you need to review every month, how to read these reports and what they actually mean. Alone, these documents, which include your balance sheet, your accounts receivable documents, and your profit and loss statements, are not that helpful. They tell you where you are, but they don't tell you where you are going. In the finance pillar, we teach you how to create something to compare them to so that it can give you context, which lets you know whether or not you are on track to reach your goals and objectives. Understanding your financial systems will help you identify how much you think you are going to bring in each month, from where, how much you think you are going to spend each month, and on what. Then you can compare your profit and loss statements to these numbers and make decisions for your business from a place of hindsight and Supreme Awareness. This level of clarity will bring you certainty in your decision-making processes and will have you making more money as if you are literally predicting and creating your financial future.

The last pillar for your business success is the **Tax Pillar.** What you learn in the tax pillar is how to save money on your taxes. Why is this important? This is important because taxes are every business owner's greatest expense. When you can save money on taxes, it's like making money because it puts money directly into your pocket. The first year I coached one of my clients and their business to a million dollars in revenue, we were extremely unprepared for the tax bill that followed. The following April my client had to come up with more than a hundred thousand dollars to pay in taxes, and he didn't have that money sitting in the bank–huge mistake! What was an even bigger mistake? We later learned that if he had done proper tax planning that year, he could've cut his taxes in half and kept $50,000 of that money in his own savings. Back then, we didn't know any of this. It took us by surprise because we weren't expecting any of this and were very surprised when it happened. How do you avoid something like this? The key is to have the right CPA on your team and to meet with your CPA more than just once a year at tax time. Once a year at tax time is simply too late. In the tax pillar we cover exactly how to choose a CPA, what taxes your business must pay, as well as what deductions your business can actually take so that when you file your taxes, you are not just looking over and missing important tax savings. You don't want to sign something that is incorrect because guess who's on the hook if you do? Let me help you with that; it is not your CPA. It is you.

Most people assume that the tax section is for people making six figures or more, which is simply not true. I had a client the other day who was making about $70,000 a year in her business. She told me that every year she pays about $10,000 in taxes, and every year she could not afford to pay them. She was building up penalties and interest, and of course, she couldn't pay that either. $10,000 in taxes on $70,000 a year is unreasonable. It's very clear to me that she's overlooking some major deductions, and if she restructured her business and her life in such a way as to maximize these opportunities, she could cut her taxes down in a big way. If you have a five-figure business, the tax pillar may be even more important for you because you can't afford to lose, to the government, the little bit of money you are bringing in.

So get ready to do a deep dive and discover the **LIFT (Legal, Insurance, Finance, and Tax)** systems that you need in place to **LIFT** your business into the stratosphere of success you desire so that you can trust and count on your business no matter what. Most importantly, so that you can put yourself out in the world in a really big way. These are the systems that will allow you, your family, your vendors, your business investors, and lenders to count on you and your business. You will be able to attract more clients because they will know that they can count on your business, and you will be comfortable in charging the higher fees that you are worth. So hang onto your hat as we do a deep dive into our **Black Wall Street Legal, Insurance, Finance, and Tax Systems** to **LIFT** your business into the stratosphere of success and beyond.

THE LEGAL PILLAR - PART 1

The goal in our **Black Wall Street Legal LIFT Pillar** is to help you establish your first foundational pillar, which includes all of the legal systems that you need in your business to succeed. This pillar is broken into two sections because there is a lot to cover in the legal foundation. The legal foundation is literally the key to everything else in your business. As the foundational pillar, this pillar can make or break your business. Before I get started, I do want to give you a quick reminder that while I am a lawyer, I am not *your* lawyer unless you paid me to be your lawyer, and we have a signed agreement to that effect. So in this role and throughout this book and course, I am here with you as your business strategist.

In many cases, you should hire a lawyer to work with you one-on-one to set up the things that we discuss in this book. I do cover what you should look for in hiring an attorney and help you identify what legal tasks you can do yourself and what you should delegate. This pillar's objectives are to give you a plan of action for exactly what you can do to get a rock-solid legal foundation as the basis for your business setup. Don't be alarmed, and don't be down on yourself if these systems and everything that I discuss in this pillar are not completed overnight. Have a little grace for yourself throughout this growth process, and note that simply gaining the knowledge and understanding of what you need to have set up will allow your creativity and growth to flow in that direction, even if only bit by bit. The growth will happen effortlessly throughout this process of stepping into a bigger reality for yourself and your business. I will go a little bit more in detail on why you need a business, although I am sure you understand that by now. I will also go into detail about where exactly that business should be based and why. By the end of this section, you will have an action plan to create the rock-solid legal foundation you need to get your business set up for optimal growth.

Why do you need a separate business entity? Boundaries. Having a separate business entity is all about boundaries. Boundaries are critical to your overall success in all areas of your life. If you lack appropriate boundaries, you end up in painful situations. That is equally true in your personal life and in business. When you have boundaries around your business, you can say *Yes* to risks that you would never say *Yes* to. And risks are absolutely critical to growing. If you can't take risks to grow your business, your business is going to be stagnant and stuck. Having a business with boundaries around it allows you to take those risks in a way that protects your personal assets. With your business set up the right way, you now have a barrier between your business activities (and business risks) and your personal assets.

So how does your business entity protect you? When you are in business, there will be disputes, disagreements, and conflicts. Anytime there is a dispute, a disagreement, or a conflict, there is a potential to have a lawsuit filed against you. You do not need to be a business entity moving around in the world afraid of being sued. When you are afraid of being sued, you play small, which means you don't put yourself out in the world in a very large way. What do we say on Wall Street? Go BIG or go home! Playing small in business is corporate suicide. The truth of the matter is, in business, there is always going to be a chance that your business may go *out of business* as your worst-case scenario. If that happens, you could end up owing a lot of people, vendors, maybe even past clients, a lot of money. You do not want to be on the hook personally for these business liabilities. This is why you need to set up a business entity and make sure you maintain that business structure over time by creating the appropriate boundaries for your business. We want you to make sure that you have the freedom in your business to walk away without personal liability for any outstanding debts. Another reason why you need to have a business entity in place is that sole proprietors are audited at a rate between five and seven times more than those who have a business entity set up the right way. I assume this is because the IRS knows that if you are a sole proprietor, you are not taking things seriously, and you are probably making some huge mistakes on your taxes. We talk about that more in the Tax Pillar, but you should know that when you have a separate business entity you are filing your taxes in a different way, which puts the IRS on notice that you are serious about your business. The third reason why you need to set up a business entity is because you get to **live the corporate lifestyle.** You can take business trips and vacations, play golf at a country club, or go to yoga on your business dime, so long as you structured your business in an appropriate way, and you are making these purchases as business expenses. In other words, as long as you are taking clients and/or business associates with you, you can *live the corporate lifestyle* on your business and on the government, which really does affect your bottom line. So again, there are two key benefits to having a separate business entity:

1. Liability protection
2. Tax protection.

Liability protection talks about the liability issues that we discussed earlier–protecting your personal assets, which allows you to take risks in your business. The tax issues are what we discussed in terms of saving on your taxes and letting you *live the corporate lifestyle.*

So let's start with liability protection. There are two types of liabilities that you should be aware of that can potentially affect your business–**inside liabilities** and **outside liabilities**. Inside liabilities are things that happen inside of your company–employee lawsuits, vendor claims against you, your clients suing you, or maybe even an employee who is driving your car and gets in an accident during work hours. All of these are inside liabilities–things that happen within your business that could create potential liability. Outside liabilities are all the things that happen outside of the bubble of protection around your business that could put your business at risk from *you*. If this is your first time hearing this, then let me say it again. ***Your business can absolutely be at risk from things that you are doing outside of your business*.** For example, let's say that you get a divorce. That could turn into an outside liability because your former spouse may say, "I am entitled to half of this business!" So now you have to go get your business valued by an accountant. You hire an accountant because now you have to buy half of that business from your soon-to-be ex-spouse. That is an outside liability that puts your business at risk because if you do not have the money to buy back your business from your former spouse, you may have to close down your business or shrink its value in some other way. Another way your business could be at risk from outside liabilities is if you have multiple businesses, which many entrepreneurs do, and you become personally liable for the assets of another business for one reason or another and now, the plaintiff is looking to your other business to satisfy that debt. This is what happens when corporate creditors from one business bleed over into your other business and try to collect monies owed. Will business number two have to satisfy the debt from business number one? Another way your business could be at risk from you is if you are in a car accident or any other situation where you could be at personal risk, or someone gets hurt in your home, and/or on your property, or on one of your rental properties. All of these things are outside liabilities that could put your business at risk.

This is where setting up your business in different states becomes a big issue because where you set your business up can impact your potential for liability. For instance, in California, as in most states, if a judgment is issued against you a creditor can come in and take your business interest away from you. In other words, if you own a business in California and a creditor receives a judgment against you, that creditor can take your business and distribute all the assets out for themselves. If your business is incorporated in a state with better asset protection laws, like Nevada, you may be able to get something called a **charging order**. A charging order says that if you own a company in a state with charging order protection and a judgment is issued against you, the creditor cannot take your membership interest in the business you own. The only thing that creditors can do is get a charging order against the company, and they will have to wait until the owner of the company agrees to distribute money in order to receive their payout. This means they are much more likely to settle with you in the event that you get a judgment because nobody wants a charging order. A charging order could mean they will have to wait until they collect your distributed assets, and in the meantime, they could be taxed on income that they will not have yet received. So in many ways, this provides an additional layer of protection because creditors do not want to get charging orders. These are very important questions to consider when thinking about where to incorporate your business. Do you want to incorporate your business in your home state? Or do you want to incorporate in a state that has charging order protections like Nevada?

Another thing to consider about where your business is conducted is the tax protections available to your business. You may have heard that in states like Nevada and Texas, there are no state income taxes. In fact, nine states — Alaska, Florida, Nevada, New Hampshire, South Dakota, Tennessee, Texas, Washington and Wyoming — have no income taxes. According to the Tax Foundation New Hampshire, however, taxes interest and dividends. (Tennessee eliminated its tax on investment income in 2021). That might sound alluring to people who live in other states, like Californians who must pay 10% of their income for state income taxes. I know what you're thinking, "I'll just start my business in Nevada." But here's the key, if you do business in your home state, and you are headquartered in your home state, and you see clients in your home state, then you have to qualify to do business in your home state. That means that your home state will tax that money even if you are incorporated in Nevada. Before you think about incorporating in another state like Nevada, for tax savings and charging order protections, you must understand that **where you actually do business** and **where business is actually conducted**, is what controls how your business is treated legally. So how do you save on your taxes by incorporating in a state like Texas if you do not live there? Obviously if you live there, you can be headquartered and conduct business there. If you do not live in Texas, you may still be able to incorporate there and take advantage of the laws.

But how? You will need to have a business that really qualifies to be headquartered in Texas and does not do business anywhere else in a specific state. For example, let's say you have a purely virtual, online internet business, a network marketing company, or a consulting business that operates in many different states and does not need to have a specific presence in any one state. You can probably incorporate your business in the state of Texas and take advantage of some of the tax laws there. The thing to ask yourself is, "Can I do my business from anywhere in the world?" If the answer is yes, then you should consider setting up your business in a state like Texas. If you want state income tax savings *and* charging order protections Nevada would be a good option. To date, only five states provide charging order protections to single-member LLCs: Alaska, South Dakota, Nevada, Delaware and Wyoming.

So again, the state tax savings question to ask yourself is, "Can my business do business anywhere in the world, including the coast of Africa, assuming I could get internet access there?" If the answer is yes, you can consider incorporating in a state like Nevada. If you do that, it would mean no state income tax, combined with charging order protection from creditors, which means you would have the best of both worlds. But this is not something you just do without reason. I am explaining this in detail because when you make this decision, I want you to make it from a place of Supreme Awareness. I want to ensure that you do it because it really makes sense for you and your business because there are additional steps that you must take. You must be headquartered in Nevada, which means you will have to use a Nevada address on everything you do in your business. This means specifically, that if you live in New York and you are headquartered in Nevada, you cannot have any New York information on your Nevada business paperwork and corporate documents. Everything has to have the Nevada address. You must be headquartered in Nevada with the phone answered there, with a bank account there, and you have to receive your mail there. You have to use the Nevada address as your mailing address, and not just a P.O. box but an actual street address. So if your business is purely virtual and you can do it from anywhere in the world, including a beach in Africa, and you do want to set up your business in Nevada, and you really do qualify because your business is purely virtual, then you pass the test and you should set up your business entity and headquarter your business in a state with charging order protections and no income tax like Nevada. If you do not meet this test, then you need to set up your business in your home state.

In every circumstance, I always advise against setting up your business entity by yourself. And please do not go to one of those inexpensive online DIY services unless you are working closely with an attorney. If you use a draft-only document assembly service without legal counsel and advice to coach you along the way, it will cost you much more money in the long run, which takes away your valuable time. Time is money, and your time should be spent on high-leverage activities like marketing, engaging clients, doing your services for your business, and growing your business. Setting up your business entity is not going to do that for you. It will be a distraction and most likely a very expensive distraction at that. As I said, I strongly urge you to hire an attorney. If your budget is not enough to hire a personal attorney to do the entire process for you, then head over to our resource center at BlackWallStreet.com for DIY resources to help you make sure you set up your business properly. Honestly, this is definitely something you should delegate if you have the money to do so.

If you are a solopreneur just getting started, and you want to put the pedal to the metal and get your business started right away, but you do not have the finances to hire an attorney, file everything yourself. As soon as your business starts generating income, hire an attorney to look over what you set up to make sure that you've done everything the right way. If you haven't already done so, head over to Black-WallStreet.com and start your black business ASAP. I don't want you to get left behind.

But before you actually start your business, you need to know what type of business entity you want to operate under. There are two main types of entities, LLC and Corporations (C-corps and S-corps). This reminds me of a question I am often asked, "Should I operate my business as an LLC, a C-corporation, or an S-corporation?" So let's talk about what these entities are. What is an LLC? What is a C-corporation? An S-corporation? And which corporate structure is better for your business?

A **C-corporation** is a legal structure for a corporation in which the owners, or shareholders, are taxed separately from the entity. The taxing of profits from the business is at both corporate and personal levels, creating a double taxation situation for its owners. A corporation is not as flexible as an LLC and is owned by shareholders. That means that if you own shares of a corporation, you are a shareholder of a corporation that is managed by its officers and board of directors. A C-corporation is the ideal business structure for a business that intends to go public on the New York Stock Exchange and raise capital through venture capitalists.

An **S-corporation** is a type of corporation where you make a selection with the government to allow all of the tax consequences to pass on to the owners personally. This selection is made by filing IRS Form 2553 and can be made by a C-corporation or an LLC.

LLC stands for **limited liability company.** With a limited liability company, you are a member of the LLC, you receive a membership interest in the LLC, and you might also be a manager of the LLC. The LLC is managed by managers and owned by members, and the governing document of the LLC is called an **operating agreement.** An operating agreement dictates how the LLC will operate, and is a very flexible document. It can say that you are the one setting up the LLC and that you are the managing member, or it can say that all members of the LLC are managing members, or that none of the other members are managing members. Unless an LLC makes an S-Corp election with the IRS, the government will look straight through a single member LLC to the owner of the company and attach those assets to the owner. In other words, they will treat a single member LLC the same way they treat a sole proprietor, and treat a multi member LLC the same way they treat a partnership for tax purposes.

Take note if you are setting up a single-member LLC. A **single-member LLC** may not give you as much asset protection as a **multi-member LLC**. While the law is clear in most states, this is still an evolving issue.

As I stated before, a creditor of an LLC member can only seek what is known as a "charging order" against the member's interest in the LLC. With a charging order, the creditor cannot directly attach the assets of the LLC, but instead receives any payments made from that member's distributional interest. With single member LLCs, there is some uncertainty as to whether creditors would be limited to a charging order since the rationale for protecting members from other members' personal debts does not apply if there is only one member. Courts in some states have found that the charging order protection doesn't apply with single member LLCs and have allowed creditors to pursue remedies, including foreclosing on the member's interest or ordering the LLC dissolved. Other states, like Nevada and Wyoming, have recently changed their laws to make clear that the charging order protection for debtors applies with all LLCs, regardless of whether they are single or multi-member entities.

If you are concerned about asset protection with an LLC, then you should have multiple members. These multiple members can be you and your spouse if you are married, which can give you the added protection that you are looking for. Just make sure that you set it up and conduct the business the right way under the law. Another method I've used is to add another partner to a single member LLC and allocate the income and expenses in different ways depending on who will receive more income and who will receive more expenses for tax purposes. Again, LLCs have a lot of flexibility–this is not something you can do with a corporation. The key is to make sure you have an operating agreement in place because this is what will govern how and under what terms the LLC will operate. This is something that you should definitely have reviewed by an attorney. You *can* do this yourself. Just make sure you have an attorney review it.

LLC v Corporation

An LLC is managed by its managers. Corporations are managed by their officers and board of directors. The profits and losses, and all of the income and expenses of a corporation, pass through in proportion to the ownership interests–there is absolutely no flexibility here.

With a corporation you cannot allocate income and expenses in any special way. Corporations are very straightforward. You do not have the same flexibility as an LLC. There is a similarity between the LLC operating agreement and a corporation's bylaws. Bylaws say how a corporation will run, when the meetings will be held, how voting will be handled, how the officers and directors will be appointed, and many other important things. So it's very important to have your by-laws reviewed by an attorney because there are some very important provisions that you may want changed based on how you want your corporation to run. Yes, you can draft your bylaws yourself. Yes, you can draft your own operating agreement, but I strongly urge you to make sure you have your documents reviewed by an attorney. Doing it yourself and having it reviewed later by an attorney will save you time and money, and it will save your attorney time so that they will bill you less.

What are the tax differences between a C-corporation, an S-corporation, and an LLC? Understanding the tax consequences of forming an LLC versus a corporation is very important because this is how you will consider which entity is right for your business. Re-member, a C-Corp is subject to double taxation. In most cases, you will want to have an S-Corp for the tax savings. For most small busi-ness owners, an LLC taxed as an S-corporation is the better business structure unless you will be owning real estate. If you are forming a company just to purchase real estate, an LLC (series LLC if the option is available in your state) is often the better structure because it's not really an operating company; it is just owning real estate, which is different than operating a business. With both an LLC and S-corps, there is no tax at the corporate level, but with an S-corporation, you can pay yourself a salary and thereby limit the amount of self-employment taxes that you pay. With an LLC, 100% of your net income will be subject to self-employment tax at a rate of 15%. Whereas with an S-corporation, all you need to do is pay yourself a reasonable salary, and the self-employment tax is **levied on your salary only and not on the rest of your income.** Your corporate requirements will depend on whether you are an LLC or C-Corp prior to making the S-corporation tax election–something to be aware of. Again, I recommend forming an LLC for flexibility with your asset protection and making an S-Corp election with the IRS to take advantage of the tax savings.

I've explained the positives and negatives of the different ways to set up a business entity. Bottom line–consult your lawyer, as well as a certified public accountant (CPA). They will guarantee you structure your business the right way to take advantage of tax deductions, etc. This reminds me of one of my favorite quotes from best-selling author Robert Kiyosaki, "Business is a team sport." Team sports require everyone playing a different position to work together to win the game. So whenever you work with a good lawyer and a good CPA, you are setting your business up for success. Your lawyer and your CPA should be talking to one another and working together to help you decide whether or not you should operate as an S-corporation or an LLC. Another thing you want to look out for in some states is high franchise taxes on the LLC that will not apply to S-corporations. As you can see, you need to consider a number of things and getting sound, professional guidance is critical.

If you choose to take advantage of the S-Corp tax election, the number one thing you must do is make sure the salary you pay yourself meets the reasonableness test. **The reasonableness test** means that you cannot pay yourself a salary of $2,000 a month if someone in a similar occupation, in a similar field, would earn $5,000 to $10,000 a month. This is definitely something that would be a red flag to the IRS.

So do you set up an S-corporation or an LLC? That depends on your unique circumstances, but in every situation, make sure you issue your membership interests. If you are issuing those interests in a corporation, you do so in the form of stock certificates that every shareholder must sign. If it's an LLC, you issue member interests through an operating agreement and/or membership certificates. Please do not leave this important step out. It's the one step that will really make your entity real on paper. With corporations, I see a lot of companies not issue their membership interest (stock certificates). They have blank stock certificates sitting in the back of their corporate binders like they do not mean anything. So please make sure you issue the membership interest in the company and make sure that it's documented in your corporate record book. After you file your paperwork with the state department of your particular state, and after you issue those membership interests, the next thing you want to do, or really you should do this simultaneously, is to obtain an EIN for your company.

Corporate entities enjoy most of the rights and responsibilities that people possess. If you think of your corporation as your baby, the EIN would be considered the baby's social security number. An **EIN** is the social security number for your business that you will get from the federal government. You should also get a **DBA**, which stands for **"doing business as,"** and you will need to get this from the local county within your particular state. The DBA will allow you to call yourself a specific business name, and if you are a sole proprietor, this may be all that you have. But if you are operating as an LLC or as an

S-corporation, I am still suggesting that you get a DBA. Why do you still need a DBA? Look at it this way. As **In the Black Resources, LLC.,** we also do business as just **In the Black Resources.** Whenever you form a business entity, you are supposed to use the Inc. or the LLC after your name, which you may not want to use for branding purposes. This is very important because to maintain your corporate shield of protection, every time you hold yourself out to the public, you must do so in a specific way; as the corporate entity in that corporate shelter, and you must put everyone on notice that you are a corporate entity so that when they do business with you, they know that they are doing business with your company and not with you individually. This is the law. But for branding purposes, you may not want to include the incorporation or the LLC in your business name. If this is the case, file your "doing business as," also known as your **Assumed Name Certificate,** with the local county in your particular state.

Sometimes you see people file multiple DBAs or Assumed Name Certificates under one LLC or incorporated business. You see this with people running multiple businesses and people with multiple streams of revenue. Best practice is to set up separate business entities instead. This will segregate the liabilities and stop one business from bleeding onto the other business. If you don't do that, if you keep all of your businesses under one business entity using multiple DBAs, or not even using multiple DBAs, you will be **commingling your corporate assets**. This is not something you want to do. It is always best practice to have separate business entities because if you commingle corporate assets, you commingle corporate risks. Whenever you have multiple business entities, it is safer to segregate your risks so that if something happens in one business, it won't bleed over and contaminate the other business. For example, looking at my own situation again, I have In the Black Resources, online business-building resources to help keep you and your bank account **In the Black, also doing business as Black Wall Street.** It is through this business that I run BlackWallStreet.com offering my corporate training courses and programs. Then I also have The Dean Law Firm, PLLC, my private law practice business that is completely separate. If something happens to The Dean Law Firm, PLLC, it will not bleed over and contaminate In the Black Resources, LLC and vice versa. So please make sure that if you have multiple businesses and multiple revenue streams, you consider whether there should be multiple business entities instead of doing everything under one business. This will also make it a lot easier if you decide to sell that business later on down the road.

Congratulations! You set up your business entity filed in the particular state of your choosing! You have a tax ID number! You have an agreement between the owners of the business, and you issued your corporate stock or your membership interest via your stock certificates or operating agreement! You are doing business and filing your tax returns every year! Are you done? Is that all you need to do? Is there anything more? Of course, there is more work to do, and the sad truth is that this is how most people run their businesses.

The most important piece to maintaining your corporate protection over time is **maintenance**. Not only must you set things up the right way, you must also **maintain compliance in order to keep that corporate shield of protection around your business over time.** So what does maintenance look like? Maintenance looks like a well-kept corporate record book. Do you have one? Where is it? What's in it? Is it full of blank pages? Have you ever added anything to your corporate record book? Have you completed meeting minutes? Have you completed your corporate resolutions? Let's do a deep dive into what should actually be inside your **corporate record book**.

If you are a corporation, you should have some initial corporate resolutions that authorize the formation of the company, setting up your bank account, your insurance, and all of the other various things that you need to start your company. You should also have notations of every action that you take that has anything to do with your company, and it should be noted in the form of a corporate resolution. For instance, if you invest in your business or if you loan money to the business, all of these things should be noted in a corporate resolution. Other things that should be noted in your corporate resolutions include when you elect officers and when you create your board of directors. Why is this important? Because one day in the future it will be time to exit your business, and you will not remember how much money you put into it, when you put it in and how the money got in there. Did you use a check? Bank transfer? These things should definitely be recorded because if not, when it's time to sell your business you will have to pay more taxes on the sale because you didn't keep good records on how much money was put into the business (to determine capital gains). So you need to keep these records in the form of your corporate resolutions.

The other thing you need to do, and I can't say this enough, is to make sure you issue your stock certificates and/or your membership interests. I can't tell you how many people I have seen over the years get these beautiful, fancy corporate books and never issue the stock certificates found in the binder. They are just blank pages sitting in the back of their corporate record book. You MUST issue those stock membership certificates because they make your business real on paper. They should say who owns the company. They should be filled out along with the stock ledger. Ideally, you want to own that stock in the name of your **living trust**. This will make it a lot easier for your loved ones if something happens to you, like incapacity or death.

The next thing you should have in your corporate binder is your bylaws or your operating agreement, which you should have reviewed by an attorney. If it is just you, and you are a solo practitioner, you can have any pre-standard bylaws or operating agreements of your choosing. But if you have a partner, the bylaws and operating agreements are the key documents that will make sure if and when something happens down the road, you can separate and exit this business as easily as possible. These documents should be customized based on the agreement you have with your business partner.

You also need to make sure you are keeping records of your annual meetings and include these records in your corporate binder. Your annual meetings are the key to ensuring that your business is being run in the right way, and here's the best part–annual meetings are tax-deductible! They can be anywhere, so have your annual meetings somewhere fun. Take a vacation and write it off. The key is to make sure you keep meeting minutes and that you are filing them away in your corporate record book. No matter what happens, whether you have a meeting or you don't, please keep a record of what happens and the meeting minutes in there. 99.9% of the time, every person who comes into my office with their corporate record book has absolutely no meeting minutes in there. Please keep your meeting minutes and make sure they are accurate and up to date.

Recap: Maintaining your corporate shield is about keeping good records. Keeping good records is how you maintain the corporate shield of protection around your business. The records are what is actually protecting you. These records are what keeps these boundaries between you and your business intact. They protect your personal assets from the liability of the business, and they are going to give you the best possible outcome in the event that you are sued and/or threatened with a lawsuit or subject to an audit. If you keep good records, you won't have to get stressed out about having to compile these records at the same time you are trying to deal with the crisis in your business. Everything will be in place, ready to serve and protect. You will know exactly what to do, and you will know exactly what you have, which will give you great insight into what your next best course of action should be. It will also prevent you from overpaying on capital gains when it comes time to sell your business.

Let me tell you a story about one of my clients. I had a client who had a business, their first business, and they put a lot of money into it, but they did not keep good records of the money that they put into the business. They did not keep these notes that I am telling you to keep in your corporate resolutions. They did not keep meeting minutes. They had no records, and they made a lot of mistakes. When they went to sell the business, they suddenly owed a lot in capital gains tax. They would probably have owed a lot less had they had records that proved how much money they actually put into the business. A **capital gains tax** is the tax that you pay on the difference between how much money you put into the business and what you ultimately sell your business for. How did that client end up owing so much money in taxes when they put in so much money early on? It's simple. They had no documentation on how much money they put into the business, and as a result, they had to pay the added taxes. You do not want to pay taxes unnecessarily, so make sure you keep good records. Keep these records in your meeting minutes. Create those corporate resolutions, and if you don't want to do it yourself, have a lawyer do it for you. Make sure that you are working with an attorney who has a system or program to keep these things updated over time, so nothing falls through the cracks later on. Ideally, you want to work with an attorney who will put you on a membership program to keep everything up to date for you and one who will not charge you an hourly rate every time you need to do something minor for your business. This way, you will not have any surprises in your business later on down the road.

Now let's discuss registered agents. Every business entity needs to have a registered agent. If you are incorporated in your home state, you can be the registered agent for your business. The **registered agent** is the person who is going to receive service of process for your business. If anybody needs to serve your business with any sort of process like a lawsuit, the registered agent is the person or business entity who would receive that service of process on behalf of the business. The registered agent will also receive all business correspondence from the state. I always recommend hiring a third-party registered agent, especially if you are doing business out of state. And the reason is this—it should not be you because what if you move? If you relocate, you may miss an important service. You want the registered agent to be stable. Someone in business to be a registered agent is as stable as it gets and will be able to receive business correspondence for you so that nothing ever gets lost and falls by the wayside. There will be no chance that you will get sued and not know about it. You cannot be a registered agent in a state you do not live in because the registered agent must reside in the state where the business is incorporated. If you are incorporated in Nevada, you will need to have a Nevada registered agent. If you are incorporated in your home state, you could be the registered agent. Even if you don't need one, I still recommend having a registered professional agent. It is not very expensive, only a couple of hundred dollars a year for someone to receive very important correspondence for you, so nothing ever falls through the crack. Having a registered agent will make sure that you never miss a lawsuit and that all correspondence regarding your company is sent to you on a timely basis.

The number one most important thing you can do to protect your personal assets from your business's activities is to never commingle your personal funds with your business's funds. Every time you put money into your business, you must treat your business like a business and keep a record of it. **Never commingle personal assets with corporate assets.** This is a very important boundary to keep around your personal life and your business. This mistake is the number one reason the court will have to *pierce the corporate veil* and treat your business entity like it doesn't exist. The court will do this because you are treating your business entity like it doesn't exist by basically running the business out of your own personal bank account. So please make sure you do not commingle assets.

How do you put money into and take money out of the business? Let's say you open your first corporate bank account (and by the way, you definitely need to have a business bank account). You take your tax ID number (EIN) from your business along with the articles of organization or your certificate of incorporation to the bank. You deposit $50,000.00 in the bank to start the business. This is personal money you put into the business. You should keep a record of this in your corporate record book via your operating agreement or corporate bylaws, through the corporate resolutions and through your meeting minutes. This is how you keep a record of you putting that money into the business. Anytime you take money out of the business, it should either come out as a salary or profit distribution to you and again, you should be keeping detailed records of this. You cannot simply spend personal money on corporate things and corporate money on personal things. This is commingling assets, which means you are NOT keeping things separate to maintain your corporate structure over time. Ideally, all corporate expenses should be made with the business debit or credit card that is in your company's name. You should use that one business debit card to purchase everything in your business to help you keep good records of how and where you are spending corporate funds. You may also want to begin building business credit by applying for and getting a corporate credit card in your business name and building a line of credit, so when you want to take out a line of credit to support your business's growth, you are able to do so. It takes money to make money, and you will likely need to invest in your business to grow it. A line of credit is a great way to do this. When you take out a corporate line of credit, as opposed to a personal line of credit, it doesn't affect your credit score even if you max out that line of credit, unlike where you have a personal line of credit, and you max that out in support of your business. If you do this, your credit score will go down. But if it's a business line of credit, you can max it out, and it does not affect your personal line of credit. Even if you personally guarantee it.

Now let's talk a little bit about personal guarantees. Make sure you don't accidentally personally guarantee business transactions and put yourself on the hook for business activities by giving yourself a personal guarantee. Yes, there are some situations where you won't be able to avoid it, but you want to try to avoid it in every situation as much as possible. So what does that mean? It means that when you sign an agreement with a client, a vendor, or with a landlord, or with anyone for that matter, make sure that you sign on behalf of the business. It should always say the name of the company and then list you as a president or CEO. Make sure every agreement you ever enter into on behalf of the company has you representing the business and not yourself personally. This will ensure the business is kept separate from you. In every agreement that you sign, look for the words "personally guaranteed" and see if you can negotiate these terms out. Maybe you will, and maybe you won't. You will at least be conscious and aware of whether or not you are personally guaranteeing a contract that you enter into on behalf of the business. I know this goes without saying, but make sure you review all documents before you sign them, and if you are not sure about something, please make sure you have that agreement reviewed by an attorney. If there is language in the contract that you are not clear on, always ask for more clarity. Inquire from the perspective of needing more clarification and not from the perspective of someone who believes they will be taken advantage of. It's not that you are looking to protect yourself from someone, but rather you are looking to minimize disagreements and disputes that may arise in the future.

Now let's discuss situations where you would want to get a personal guarantee from someone else. Whenever you are contracting with someone who will owe you money, as in a payment plan where you are selling something and the customer will be making payments over time, or a coaching program where customers are making payments over time, or a consulting agreement that will be fulfilled over time. Anytime someone is receiving a service or a product but not paying for it in full upfront, make sure you get a personal guarantee. If you just enter into an agreement with an LLC or a corporation, and you send them a whole bunch of your products and services, you will not be able to collect the money owed if the company doesn't have any assets for you to collect. If you get a personal guarantee, it is much more likely that you can collect because you will be able to collect from their personal assets like their next paycheck, for instance. Whenever you are selling something on a payment plan or delivering a service or a product before being paid in full, consider yourself the bank and get the same information that a bank would get if they were lending money to someone. You would want to know things like their business name, their business structure, whether or not they are an LLC or a corporation, and their tax ID number. This will make it so much easier for you to collect your money if they decide not to pay you.

Something else you should watch out for in business is your social security number. I am not talking about protecting your social security number in the sense of protecting yourself from identity theft, although you should be protected there too. The kind of protection I'm talking about is to protect your personal social security number from your business. You want to protect your social security number from somebody running your personal credit when they should be looking into your business credit. Inquiries on your credit report hurt your credit score significantly, as much as three to five times—sometimes up to seven points. In today's economy, that can make a huge difference on your ability to borrow money and at what rate you can borrow. This is why you really want to protect your credit score. If someone is going to need your credit or need your social security number on something, it probably means you are personally guaranteeing it. Whenever someone is asking for your social security number, you should always ask, "Why?" This is not something you should be afraid of. This is part of putting personal boundaries in place, and it's perfectly okay for you to ask these questions. It's not about being combative and antagonistic. It's about making sure you are protected. Remember, you are never too busy, too proud, or too shy to ask why. Take the time, ask why, and ensure that you do everything with Supreme Awareness and your consciousness on high alert.

Earlier I stated that we would touch on what you can do on your own in your business and what you should be delegating. This is where I want you to think about where you should focus your creative genius and where you should be spending your time and energy to yield the highest return on your investments, where you should be investing in your business, and whether or not your activities are the highest and best use of your time. If you are just getting started and have no money, you may have no other option than to do it yourself online. Visit our DIY resources at BlackWallStreet.com and set up your business entity yourself. Make sure you watch a few of our video tutorials so that you are guided through the process step-by-step. And as soon as you start making a little money, hire a lawyer to make sure you are set up the right way. Make sure it is a lawyer who is not going to nickel and dime you and bill you out on an hourly basis. What you need is an attorney with a monthly membership program so that you can call and ask them all kinds of questions about your business and get all of your legal agreements and documents reviewed without having to worry about being charged on an hourly basis.

I wouldn't use a CPA to set up my business entity either because the CPA is not going to guide you through the agreements, counsel you on your employment issues, on your branding issues, on your copyright and trademark issues, and most CPAs are going to do the same thing that you would do. They are just going to go online and set it up and forget it. So make sure you are setting things up with a professional, and I believe that professional should be an attorney. If you are not going to set things up with a professional, you can go online and do it yourself. If you are going to set up your business entity yourself, make sure to get your tax ID number, you get your operating agreement or your bylaws in place, you fill up your corporate record book with all of your stock certificates or membership interests, and that you document business activities using minutes and corporate resolutions. Do not leave this stuff empty! This is the stuff that will actually make your business entity real. As soon as you get some money in the bank, have all of these documents reviewed by an attorney. If you already have a business entity in place, have them take a closer look at it. Has it been set up the right way? Are you in compliance? If you got sued today or threatened with a lawsuit, would you be able to trust your records because everything is set up the right way? Do you feel confident and secure that your personal assets are not at risk? If not, then these are the things that you should get taken care of ASAP. This is what should be included in your action plan. Make a decision as to how you are going to get this stuff taken care of, and just do it! Are you going to contact one of the attorneys on Black Wall Street and schedule a **Black Wall Street LIFT Your Black Business Audit,** or are you going to do this audit yourself? What is your next step?

Before we get into agreements, employee issues, and branding issues, I want to make sure that you have the entity part taken care of because this is the foundation of your business. Please make a commitment to yourself that you are going to get these things set up and fixed right away. This is your first call to action. I understand if this feels a bit overwhelming. You may want to break these things down step-by-step and take everything one day at a time. Rome wasn't built in a day, and neither were the pyramids. Be sure to head over to BlackWallStreet.com to find business resources designed to help you minimize the distance from where you are today and where you want to be.

By now, you should have a complete understanding of the three main entity types that you may want to use, either a limited liability company (LLC), C-corporation or S-corporation, how to separate yourself from your business, protect your assets and protect your credit score. You should have already decided where your entity will be based and why you are basing it there, and what you need to do to fix up your entity if you didn't do these things the right way the first time. Setting things up the right way the first time will give you a rock-solid legal foundation for success. Make sure you note your action steps here. You will either hire an attorney to do that for you, or you can do it on your own using our **Black Wall Street LIFT Business Audit.** We will talk more about the financial systems that you need in place in the financial section of the **Black Wall Street LIFT Pillar.**

Please remember to check out BlackWallStreet.com for additional resources because black wealth is critical to black power. You will find extensive checklists and DIY course to make sure your corporate entity and your corporate books are set up properly. You can simply go through the checklist and check off each box every time something is done to make things easier for you.

Last but not least, we should discuss junk mail. Junk mail is often sent to you after you file your incorporation, and it is from people who are trying to trick you into sending money to them–money you do not have to send. Be sure to take a look at what you receive in the mail so that you don't fall for any of these traps. If you want a step-by-step walk-through guide on how to set these things up the right way, head over to BlackWallStreet.com. Once you get your corporate records all set up, make sure you put them in your Black Wall Street Digital Corporate Binder so that you have all of your legal documents in one place. As soon as you've done all that, head over to the next chapter where we talk about agreements and employee issues, branding, copyrights, trademarks, and all of the other legal things that make your business work.

THE LEGAL PILLAR - PART 2

In this section, we will discuss the remaining legal tasks you need to complete to have your business set up on a rock-solid foundation. In the last chapter I covered why you should have a business entity, where that business entity should be located, and how to get that business entity set up to protect your personal assets from your corporate activities. If you already have a business entity set up, you learned how to fix it so that it's set up properly. We also discussed how to avoid inadvertently personally guaranteeing anything and leaving yourself on the hook for things that should be covered by your business. In this section we will do a deeper dive into corporate agreements and what they actually should look like.

Corporate Agreements

Here at BlackWallStreet.com we view agreements as the perfect opportunity for you to gain clarity about your business relationship. Agreements are used to make sure that we have a meeting of the minds about particular issues that may arise between contracting parties. So who do you need to have an agreement with? You need to have an agreement with anybody and everybody that you are doing business with. Instead of seeing legal agreements as a legal construct concocted to make your life more difficult, you should view agreements as an opportunity to clarify your vision to know whether or not you are on the same page with everyone that you are working with. You can have an oral agreement or a written agreement, but because oral agreements are a lot harder to prove, you should write your oral agreements down on paper as soon as time permits. This is the best way to know that you and the other party are on the same page, in addition to minimizing the risk of disagreements and disputes of any kind in the future. Think of it this way. You have two really good people with two really good intentions (actually great intentions) and they want to do right by each other. One party believes that they are supposed to do this, and the other party believes that they are supposed to do that. What they don't see, and what they do not understand, is that they are never quite on the same page. They thought they were, so they jumped right into the project investing money and a significant amount of time and effort into their venture to make it successful. Out of nowhere they have a disagreement, and now they are conflicted. Without something written down on paper to revert back to, this situation would likely end up in court. And the agreement they have is a lot more difficult to prove because, with an oral agreement, you have to first prove to the court what terms the parties actually agreed to *before* the court can consider if a breach of those terms (breach of contract) occurred. The court may also find that the parties never really agreed to anything at all. This is why it is always best practice to write your agreements down. These agreements do not have to be complicated or complex, but they should be memorialized (written down). Having agreements will bring more harmony and ease into your life and into your relationships.

What types of agreements do you need to have for your business? The first agreement, and we touched on this in the previous chapter, is an **Operating Agreement** if you are operating as an **LLC** or **Bylaws** if you are operating as a **C-corporation**. This agreement must be in writing, signed by all parties, and be included in your corporate record book. The majority of people, especially solopreneurs, leave these documents blank. But if you are in a partnership with someone in the form of an LLC or a C-corporation, make sure you customize these documents to the facts and circumstances of your business. Remember, business is a team sport, and people do business with people they know, like, and trust. One of the most important decisions you will make as a business owner is who you chose to do business with. This is an interesting topic for me because last year in America, racial tensions rose to an all-time high. Many people of color were upset with White America because they saw themselves as victims of racial discrimination, which interfered with their ability to get work and/or find viable business opportunities.

Do you remember the original Black Wall Street? You cannot be victimized by white supremacy if you learn how to create your own opportunities. It doesn't matter to me whether or not White America supports me. I believe there is a community for everyone. I founded BlackWallStreet.com to support and uplift the black community. I founded the new Black Wall Street for you. Walk in your authenticity, and those who love you and who want to do business with you and those who you should actually be doing business with will vibrate into your experience. It is law.

One very important thing you should know about partners, however, is that this will be one of your biggest potential areas for conflict and problems in your business. A partner could be anyone–someone you are married to, a boyfriend, a girlfriend, a friend, or it can be someone who is purely a business partner. Whenever you are in a partnership with someone, you have to think about how you are going to exit that partnership, and you need to have this discussion and enter into these agreements at the beginning of the relationship, not when the problems appear. The more thought you put into this ahead of time, the easier things will be for you later on.

You have to go into every partnership assuming that at some point, you will exit. What would happen if one of the partners becomes incapacitated or dies? Will you then be in partnership with that person's heirs, like their spouse, partner, or children? Is there going to be a way for you to buy out your partner's interest? All of these answers would be documented in what is called a buy-sell agreement. To put it simply, a **Buy-Sell Agreement** lays out exactly what would happen if one of the partners wants out of the agreement or if one of the partners dies or becomes incapacitated. Yes, you are building a business today so that you can serve your clients, but you are also building a business so that one day your business will be able to provide you with the freedom and security of living without you having to do every single thing within that business. That may mean that you will sell the business or stay on as owner of the business and have someone else run the business on a day-to-day basis. Regardless of the scenario, what you need to be thinking about is what will be your exit plan because I can assure you that you will not want to be in your business forever. I guess some people do, but truth be told, you know deep down inside that you do not want to run your business forever.

The more thought you put into your exit plan now, in the beginning stages of growing your business before you want to exit, the better it will be for you in the long run–**and it must be documented.** So again, you need to have a buy-sell agreement anytime you are in partnership with someone. And that goes for any partnership, even if it is a marriage (in marriage, it is called a **prenuptial agreement**).

Most people have very negative thought patterns when it comes to prenuptial agreements. Most people believe that a prenuptial agreement is what you put in place because you are planning for divorce. In some cases, that may be true, but not in all. The way that you should consider a prenup, or a buy-sell agreement, is that it's really about planning so that both of you have the best possibility of maintaining a happy relationship at the point when, and if, you realize that you no longer want the relationship to be the same as it was in the beginning. So consider it. What would happen if you or your partner wanted to exit the business? Who would be running the business from that point on? Who would want to buy a partner out? How would you buy your partner out? How would the business be valued? All of this should be documented in a buy-sell agreement. You really should talk to an attorney about this because creating your own buy-sell agreement can be tricky as it can be structured in a number of ways. For example, you may want to build into your agreement how your business will be valued. Will it be valued by an appraiser? Will each of you pick an appraiser, and then a third appraiser comes in who is picked by those appraisers to value the company? If the company is going to be valued at, let's say, $500,000, that would mean that you would have to come up with $250,000 to buy your partner out. Where is that money going to come from? Another thing you must consider is will the buy-sell agreement be funded with insurance so that in the event of a death of one of the partners, the insurance is available for the other partner to buy out the family of the partner who died?

Let's take a look at what this might look like. As I said before, we have a company together valued at $500,000, half a million dollars, and now one of us passes away. Well, let's say I die, and you want to buy out my children who will take over the company because they now own my interest in the company, which I left to them in my will. You want to buy out my children because you don't want to be in business with my children. How are you going to come up with $250,000? If there's insurance on my life, **Key Man Insurance**, also referred to as **Buy-Sell Insurance**, then the insurance would payout directly to you or directly to the company for the sole purpose of buying out my heirs. So if you are going to have a **Buy-Sell Agreement**, which you should, then you should consider how you will actually fund that buy-sell agreement with insurance. To be clear, this insurance is not going to be triggered if one of you just wants to get out of the company, which is also something to consider. But again, that is something that you'll work through in your agreement with one another. Make sure that you understand and think through what would happen if one of you wants to exit the business.

Another very important agreement that you will need for your business is an agreement with your vendors (**Vendor Agreement**). You also need agreements with your clients (**Client Agreements**) and **Confidentiality Agreements/Non-disclosure Agreements** if you will be sharing information about your company with other people. You may also need some **Media Release Forms**. I promise to do a deep dive into these types of agreements later on in this chapter.

Another type of agreement you may need is an **Affiliate Agreement** or **Joint Venture Agreement**. What is the difference between an affiliate and a joint venture? An **affiliate relationship** is one in which a person is just a sales agent for somebody else's products. For example, if we enter into an affiliate relationship where you offer my products to people that you know, and you receive a commission for those sales. You are not my representative or a representative of my company. We have no formal relationship other than that of you selling my products to your friends, family, clients, colleagues, fans, and following. That is an affiliate relationship. On the other side of this is a joint venture relationship, which is much more substantial. A **joint venture relationship** is not simply you promoting my product to your list; it's you and I coming together and pooling our resources and together offering a product, program, or service. What I find with most joint venture relationships is that they are not documented properly. At the very bare-bones minimum, you should at least have a documented email exchange between you and the other person that you are doing the joint venture with, which clarifies the terms of your agreement. For instance, "*It says here what I am going to do. It says here what you are going to do, and here's how we're going to split any money that comes in from this venture". This is how we're going to pay for this venture and who's going to put the money in, and under what circumstances.* The key is to look at every joint venture relationship that you are entering into and determine how valuable and important it is. If it is very important and valuable to you, you want to get a lawyer involved in drafting your joint venture agreement. At the bare minimum, at least talk about who's doing what and under what circumstances each of you will put money in, and how you will split the money that comes out on the other side. Please write it down, even if it is just in the form of an email. In a simple affiliate relationship you may not need that. A simple affiliate agreement would say that the affiliate is representing your product and that they are going to comply with any terms of the affiliate program and say exactly how much they are going to receive as an affiliate and when they'll receive those affiliate payments.

I mentioned earlier what you can do yourself and what you should delegate to someone else. When you have a simple joint venture relationship that is not that valuable to you, you can send a simple email to memorialize how you and someone will be working together. In this scenario, a bare minimum email to memorialize your agreement is a great way to go. Send that email and quickly document your agreement. Email is one of the best inventions of our generation because it allows us to communicate extremely fast, which makes it a great way to document your agreements. When you enter into an agreement with someone, shoot them a quick email that says, "Just to confirm that we're both on the same page, here's what I understand we are agreeing to." Then lay out the terms of what you agree to. At the bottom, say, "If you agree, please send me back an email letting me know that you agree to these terms. If anything requires clarification, shoot me back an email letting me know what we need to clarify before we determine that we are going to move forward and take any actions." Then you go back and forth a couple of times, making any adjustments before you confirm that you are on the same page, or you may get a quick email back that says, "Yep, we're on the same page." This is the easiest way to document your agreements, and it is free to use every single time. It is very non-emotional and non-threatening. You do not need an attorney to do this for you, but of course, please be as specific as possible and really trust your intuition on this. In other words, understand what your limits and boundaries are from a subconscious level. And have a backbone. I know a lot of women in business tend to wimp out when it comes to stating their demands, but the clearer your demands are and knowing what your bottom line is and knowing what the other person's bottom line is, and being very clear from the start will ensure that you have a happy relationship down the line.

What about intentions? My grandmother always said, "The road to hell is paved with good intentions." When I began my journey in entrepreneurship, one of my pet peeves was meeting with other entrepreneurs to discuss business ideas and deals and never consummating those deals. There was all of this talk about our intentions and what we intended to do. Let me make this very clear. Intentions are not the same as agreements. When you require firm agreements and not intentions, people will take you seriously in your business *and* your life. Period. When you do decide to raise money for your company in any way, whether through investors or lenders, you will be able to show them that you take your business seriously. You will have documented agreements that will show your transaction records and things that you've done in your business, and it will help show that you are building a business people can really count on.

You will hear me say this over and over again. Business is a team sport, and you need a team. We are now going to talk a little bit more about your employees and independent contractors because these are both your biggest help, as well as your biggest potential for danger. This is where you will most likely get sued, but on the flip side, you cannot grow without them. You simply cannot build a business without support, without having a team. Your employees and independent contractors are the team members you hire to support you. One thing you should know before you start hiring is that there are certain protected classes of people. This means that whenever you are advertising for any sort of position, you cannot discriminate on the basis of race, gender, age, pregnancy, medical, disability, or religion. Make sure there's nothing in your advertising for the employment position that will lead someone to believe you are discriminating against one of these protected classes. You may also want to watch your questioning during the interview process when you are hiring this person. We have a document provided at BlackWallStreet.com called an **Employment Policies and Procedures Checklist**. This document will help you to do a deep dive into your interview process to make sure you are not violating any of these rules. Check that out, especially those of you who have a virtual business. You might inadvertently violate a discrimination law by asking something about children, such as making sure they will not have kids running around in the background. Instead, you may want to ask, "Do you have a quiet space to work where you are not interrupted?" You can absolutely require that whoever is working for you from their home have a quiet space to work where they are not interrupted. You cannot require that they not have children because that would violate one of the discrimination laws. That would be discriminatory. To be compliant, you need to focus on specific policies rather than specific situations.

You should make a list of all the things you need in your business and all the things you are looking for in a person. What's great about making this list is that it not only helps you with employment from a hiring perspective, but it will also help to make sure that you find the right person from a conscious perspective. This is a great place to use the law of attraction in your business. Get crystal clear about the qualities and attributes that you are looking for in your ideal team member and write them all down. Just like they tell you to do in the documentary, *The Secret*, which teaches about the law of attraction. Clarity is where success starts, so write it all down. You will be able to match up whoever comes in for an interview with your desired attributes.

I definitely recommend providing your prospective employees and prospective team members with a job application that will ask them things that you may not think to ask during the interview process. You can also find a sample **employment application** for you at our resource center at BlackWallStreet.com. **A word of caution:** If you are hiring independent contractors, you do not want your independent contractors to sign employment applications. This will make it seem as though they are actually your employee and not an independent contractor. This is very important because you do not want to have your team members misclassified. That will get you into a lot of trouble, especially with the IRS. What you could potentially do is create a **vendor application** or run a background check to get around that. We like to use an application because there are going to be things that you want to put in the application. Things like, "Have you ever been convicted of a felony?" and other things you may want to know before hiring someone and taking them on as a potential vendor.

While we are talking about hiring, we should also talk about **employee versus independent contractor issues**. This is a huge issue, and many people are doing it incorrectly. The reason why it's such a big issue is that with an employee, you pay half of the employee's payroll taxes at about 7.5%, and they pay half of their payroll taxes, the other 7.5%. But when someone is an independent contractor, at the end of the year, you give them a 1099 instead of a W-2, and they pay their own employment taxes and their own payroll taxes at about 15%. So that saves you quite a bit of money. If you incorrectly classify someone as an independent contractor, and they are really an employee, and they do not pay their taxes, guess what? You are the one who is responsible for those back taxes. **Proper classification of your team members is extremely important.**

What about virtual team members? Just because someone is working virtually does not automatically make them an independent contractor. Of course, there are boundaries and things that you can do to make sure a team member is an independent contractor, but, again, just because they are virtual does not automatically make them one. The standard has more to do with control and whether or not they are working for themselves or for you. The less control you exercise, the more likely someone is considered an independent contractor. In fact, as independent contractors, they need to be exercising independent discretion on how they carry out their job. They should be using their own equipment. They should be able to work on your job whenever they want to, however long they choose to, and they determine when they get the job done. I cannot overemphasize this enough–**You must have in place an independent contractor agreement for anybody who is working with you in a non-employee capacity**. And of course, you can also find an independent contractor agreement at BlackWallStreet.com. In many cases, if you work with a real professional as a virtual assistant or a vendor, they will have their own independent contractor agreement for you to sign. It's really important that you make this classification properly because if you do not, you could be responsible for back taxes, and you could also be on the hook for overtime and break time. Employees are required to be given a certain amount of break time every day, and they must be paid overtime. So please make sure that you are classifying your team members correctly.

In our resource center at BlackWallStreet.com, we also have a work-for-hire agreement. When you use a **Work-For-Hire Agreement** for someone that you are getting some business from on a work-for-hire basis, typically an independent contractor, you should make sure that you include the correct work for hire clauses in that agreement. This is a huge area where many people make a lot of mistakes. For example, if you hire someone to build you a website, you most definitely need to put a work-for-hire agreement in place. If you do not put a work-for-hire agreement in place, that web development team will own the source code of the software that you two developed together, even though it was your idea and your money, and even though you invested your time, ideas, and energy. This is so because, **as a general rule, every independent contractor and every single person owns what they create.** To make sure that *you* own what they are creating for you, you will need to have a specific clause stating that fact in your work-for-hire agreement. On the flip side, if you are a graphic designer, web developer, or another creative type, you need to make sure you have a provision in your work-for-hire agreement that says you own all of the intellectual property rights of what you are creating until you are paid in full. This will ensure that you always get paid in full and that your clients are not able to take what you've worked so hard to create without paying you. Make sure that you own the copyright. You should own that intellectual property until you are paid in full. As you can see, these agreements work both ways as everybody needs these clauses on both sides of the table.

Another thing to discuss is **offer letters**. If you are hiring someone as an employee or independent contractor, I recommend giving them an offer letter that makes it perfectly clear what their duties are, what their pay will be, whether they are an employee or an independent contractor, and what you expect from them. Make sure that the offer letter states that their employment will be at-will. **At-Will Employment** is where an employee can be fired at any time, for any reason, without any notice. In the offer letter, you also want to say that the terms cannot be changed by any oral representation and that they cannot be changed without written notice and consent. It should also say that the terms and conditions of their employment are only the ones written into the offer letter, and there is nothing else that exists in the universe of this employment, including any oral statements, that governs the terms and conditions of their employment. You may also want to include in your offer letter a statement that this is only good so long as the references check out, the background check checks out, and the credit check checks out. When you do this, there is no risk that somebody would be able to come back later on and say, "Well, you told me 'this,' and therefore, we have an agreement." It all needs to be written down and made very clear that nothing else would be able to supersede what is there in writing. You can also find a sample offer letter online at BlackWallStreet.com.

As you are going through the hiring process, you should consider running credit and background checks, in which case you will want to work with a background check company. If you will be running credit checks, you must comply with a federal law called the Fair Credit Reporting Act. In California, it is the California Consumer Reporting Act, and you may have a different one in your state. California is pretty strict. To run a background check in California, you have to make an offer of employment contingent on running a background check. For example, you will have to say specifically in your offer letter that this offer is only good so long as your references check out, the background check checks out, and the credit check checks out so that the employment is contingent upon the background check. In New York, you are able to conduct a background check, but New York places certain restrictions on how employers may use this information in their employment decisions.

For example, employers are only permitted to inquire about convictions rather than arrests or charges that did not lead to a conviction. Employers are also prohibited from denying employment unless 1.) there is a direct relationship between the conviction and the employment sought, and 2.) granting the employment would involve an unreasonable risk to property or the safety or welfare of others. This requires employers to analyze the conviction by applying factors instead of just making a blanket rule decision. Typically, you see this requirement across the board. There must be a reasonable relationship between whatever it is that the party is convicted of and any kind of credit irregularity in the actual job. This is really important to know. So, for instance, if someone is late on their mortgage, but being late on their mortgage does not have any reasonable relationship to the position that they are applying for, you cannot use this as a reason not to hire that person. If you are running background checks and credit checks on potential candidates and you decide not to hire someone as a result, make sure to speak with an attorney so that whatever it is that came up is a reasonable reason to not hire that person. Otherwise, you could get yourself in a lot of trouble. You always, always, always want to make sure you check references. This is a critical piece that many people skip because they are just overwhelmed and think the other person seems nice. But do not be fooled; you must always check references. The questions you always ask when checking references are, "Is this person eligible for rehire?" and "Would you hire them back?" When I check references, I am always trying to get as much information as I can get.

Legally, the person giving the reference is not allowed to give out certain information, but that doesn't mean that they will not, and it doesn't hurt to ask. Today, many companies just simply will not give out any information other than whether or not the person is eligible for rehire, but that does not mean you can't ask. The person you should call is the direct supervisor of the employee. Don't just call human resources because the human resources person may not even know the employee or the independent contractor you are thinking of hiring. You always want to call and talk to a direct supervisor. Whenever possible, you always want to talk to someone who actually knows the person you are hiring. You want to ask as many questions as possible, as many questions as you feel like asking, knowing that they may not be able to answer all of them - but they might. Sometimes people just like to give out a lot of information. One of my favorite questions to ask is, "Is there anything that I should know before hiring this person?" It's an open-ended question that gives the person room to talk, and affords you an opportunity to listen to what they have to say. In any event, you always ask whether or not they would rehire this person.

Now let's discuss the **Employee Handbook**. This is an important document because it's all of the written policies and procedures about working for your company. You want to have your handbook reviewed by an employment lawyer in your state. You can find a sample employee handbook at BlackWallStreet.com. Generally, employee handbooks are pretty inexpensive. Many employment lawyers will have standard employee handbooks that you can purchase, which they can then customize for you. In any event, your handbook should include notices like: employees should not have any reasonable expectation of privacy on their computers, their voicemail, and in their emails, basic things that are standard in every policy and procedure handbook or employee handbook.

You need to get that taken care of for your business specifically. You will need to include things like vacation time, sick time, etc. It's important to have your handbook reviewed by an attorney in your state because every state has different employment laws, things like whether or not you have to provide vacation or sick time. If you do, how do you do this? You don't want to accidentally violate one of these and then end up owing all sorts of back pay for someone who did not take vacation or sick time. Really make sure you get this reviewed by an employment attorney in your state because there may be a lot of state-specific terms and laws that you want to be on the lookout for. One thing you should absolutely have in your employee handbook is a statement that says, "No employees can work overtime without written authorization from their supervisor." This will keep you safe from the next thing we need to discuss, which is wage and hour violations. **This is the biggest place you are likely to be on the hook if you have an employee.** You need to know what the laws are in your state regarding wage and hour requirements.

How many hours a day can a person work without being entitled to overtime? How many hours in a week can they work? You should also be keeping track of their time. They need to clock in and clock out, and if they refuse to clock in and out, you need to write them up. These methods may sound a bit draconian, but they are exactly what is needed to protect you from lawsuits and litigation. I know this from firsthand experience. I had a really nice client who had employees that he was very loose with. They did not have to clock in. They did not have to clock out. They could work whenever they wanted. This is exactly what got him into trouble with wage withholding and hour violations. Make sure that you are getting timesheets from your employees, and if they refuse, write them up. This can be a problem where many small business owners get in trouble because they are simply not keeping good employee records. If you are not keeping good records, the presumption is always against you. The presumption is that your employees *did* work that overtime, and they did not take breaks. Of course, that is what they will say when they sue you. Make sure you have your employees keep track of their time, no matter how much they complain about having to do it.

Writing people up and keeping employees accountable is usually among your least favorite parts of the business. But if you are a small business, you likely don't have a human resources department. It is very important to review your employees at least once every quarter regularly, and when they are new, once a month. You do not want these problems to build up. For example, do not wait for there to be five problems, and then you fire them. You need to have consistent, documented records that you gave them warnings, that you tried to help them improve, and then, only after that is when you terminate someone. You cannot simply have a conversation with a difficult employee and say, "It seems like you are having trouble sometimes–how can I help you?" You must document everything. And make sure that you are doing employee reviews, documenting these reviews, and not just allowing their behavior to continue because you are a nice person. I know you are a nice person. We are all nice people. I trust that your employees will also know that you are a nice person, but when it comes to human resources, you need to set some very clear boundaries and be the boss. That is what it means to take your business seriously and to really show up and build your business for success.

I think we can all agree that when it comes to terminating someone, this is probably the worst part of your job, but you do have to be strict about your business to be successful. When you terminate someone, it is very important to understand that the people working for you are not your friends. At BlackWallStreet.com we say, "Hire slow and fire fast!" Build a 90-day trial period into every new hire position with your company. This statement embodies one of the most important decisions you'll ever make for the growth of your company. If you fail to do this, your unemployment insurance may go through the roof because you'll be bringing people in and letting them go very quickly, and then they may want to collect unemployment. Instead, build a 90-day trial period and get to know someone and how they work with your company. Conduct weekly reviews during this trial period to really determine whether they are a good fit, and listen to your intuition. You will know right away whether someone is working out or not. You can tell by their attitude. You can tell by how quickly they pick things up. If they are not a good fit, let them go and make room for the person who is going to come in and do a fantastic job. If you are holding onto baggage, you are blocking your blessings. You are blocking the person who is a perfect fit for you and your company by holding on to someone who just is not right for your business.

Employment Action Steps: Now, let's cover a few action steps in terms of employment.

1. Make sure to utilize the checklist on how to set up the right employment policies and procedures in the right way and

avoid costly mistakes that you will find in our companion course at BlackWallStreet.com.

2. Create a list of your ideal characteristics and traits for each of your team members.

3. Create an organizational chart. An **organizational chart** is a document that lays out all the various team members that you need, who is reporting to who, and who will give you clarity about the roles that you need to fill in your company. You can find some sample organization charts at Black-WallStreet.com.

Intellectual Property

Now it's time to do a deep dive into intellectual property. For many small business owners, intellectual property is really about protecting their brand. As a small business owner, your brand is the absolute most important asset that you have, next to your trade secrets. Everything else can come and go, but your brand name is the core of your business and how people will find you, which also includes your brand reputation. Ensure that you have a strong brand to begin with and that you are in a good position to make sure no one else can leverage the work you've put into building your brand. A lot of people really don't understand how to name their company in a way to protect their brand. Let's look at what happened to my **LIFT** mentor, Alexis Martin Neely. She named one of her first companies, The Personal Business Family Lawyer. When she went to trademark this name with the USPTO (United States Patent and Trademark Office), she was denied. They said her name was not trademarkable because it merely described a type of lawyer, a personal-business-family lawyer, as opposed to being distinguishable. She later found out that she could get a U.S. trademark for this, but it was on a secondary register called the supplemental register. What is the supplemental register? The **supplemental register** is a secondary list maintained by the USPTO for marks that do not qualify for the principal register. Here, you have five years to build a brand around that trademark to make it distinguishable to your business. That's how she got the trademark for The Personal Family Business Lawyer. She was able to use the ® symbol, and in five years, she was able to go back and say, "Look, my brand is not just describing a type of lawyer. I built a whole brand around this term, personal-family-business lawyer." She eventually got it, but it had to sit on the supplemental register for five years first. Not all names can be protected, but chances are you will be able to get it put on the supplemental register and prove that you are building a brand around it. Do not just abandon the trademark if you get a response from the trademark office that says, "Sorry, that name is not trademarkable."

Is a trademark, DBA, and domain name the same thing? No; but they can be. A **domain name** is registered on the worldwide web so that there is an internet address. A business's assumed name (**DBA-Doing Business As**) is registered to identify a business that wishes to conduct business in a name that is different from its incorporated name. Take BlackWallStreet.com for instance. I purchased this piece of digital real estate for [1]$75,000.00 because I believe *Black Wealth is Critical to Black Power*. I built a whole brand around this domain. I also have a DBA for In the Black Resources, LLC to do business as Black Wall Street and BlackWallStreet.com, but is this enough to make Black Wall Street our trademark? What exactly is a trademark?

---

[1] BlackWallStreet.com domain purchase receipt at the end of book

What names can you trademark? our trademark? What exactly is a trademark? What names can you trademark?

A **trademark** protects the investment that you've put into your name and/or your company's logo. When you file the application to register your trademark, you cannot simply describe the goods or services. This is not enough because there is a cognitive gap that has to be filled, and you fill this cognitive gap with marketing. The goal with your brand name is to get an emotional element that is suggestive of what you are selling. A test I like to use is called the "What is that?" test. For example, if you give someone your business card where you are the president of a hair and nail company, and your business card says Mary's Hair and Nails, they will know exactly what you do. That is not distinctive enough to be a trademark because it is merely descriptive like the trademark office said my mentor's personal family business lawyer brand was. Now let's say you are the president of a company called Wood and Pencil, which is an actual company by the way. And when you see Wood and Pencil, the first thing that pops in your mind is, "What kind of businesses is that?" When you have that question, this means that you have enough of a gap. You fill in this gap with marketing, or at least a conversation, a brochure, a logo, or something else to let the consumer know exactly what it is that you do. Understanding this will help you tremendously from a trademark perspective.

Anytime you put your brand out there, make sure to protect it by always using the trademark symbol (™), which means that you are staking your claim on this particular brand. It does not cost you anything to do this. You just put it on your brand, and that stakes your claim. If you want to step it up a notch, you should register that brand so that you can use the registered trademark symbol (®). You register your trademark by filing an application with the USPTO. Once registered, that is the U.S. Patent and Trademark Office giving you their seal of approval on your brand, saying, "This brand is distinctive enough to have a trademark, and you are the first person to use this brand in commerce." Why register your trademark with the USPTO? Doing so will give you a presumption of validity if you ever have to enforce your mark or to make someone stop using your mark. Because the first thing the attorney on the other side will say when you question their mark is, "That is not your mark, and you are not the first person to start using it." If you have the (®) symbol, meaning you registered that trademark, then they will not be able to invalidate your claim. If you do not have the mark registered, then there will be a discussion followed by a dispute that will probably end up in a court of law. So the goal in this legal part of our **Black Wall Street LIFT Pillar** is to minimize disputes and minimize the cost of these disputes that may arise in the future.

One of the scariest things you'll ever have to face as a business owner is receiving a letter from someone saying that you are infringing on their brand name. So before you brand something and put the (™) symbol on it, and before you invest a whole lot of money in creating any sort of product, program, or service, you need to search and determine whether someone else has already filed a trademark application or registered that trademark because you never want to get the letter of doom in the mail. The letter I am referring to is a **Cease and Desist Letter,** which will cost you a lot of money to deal with. You may need to hire an attorney. You may have to rebrand everything. These are all expenses you do not want to incur and expenses you can very easily avoid by merely doing research at the beginning of your business to determine whether or not someone else has already filed a trademark application on the brand name you are looking to do business with.

What's the difference between a **trademark** and a **copyright**? A **trademark** protects the investment in your brand, and **copyright** protects the expression of your creativity. But what exactly does that mean? For example, copyrights protect your website, copy, and your graphic design for your brochures, but it does not protect your ideas. As a matter of fact, ideas are never protected. Copyright protects what you create with those ideas, and you want to make sure that you are registering your copyrights. If you are in the creative business as an artist or entertainer, and part of your job is creating new information or writing copy, you should have business systems in place to consistently register your copyrights. The fee is only $35 online. You can do this yourself, and this is something you should do as part of your standard business operations. You should register your copyrights because if you ever need to pursue a claim, you can recover punitive damages against the person who stole your copyright if you are not paid. **Punitive damages** are damages that are awarded to you simply to punish the other party. This can mean the difference between being able to collect on payment and not being able to collect on payment.

If you do not register your copyrights and someone uses your work without paying you, it will be a lot more expensive for you to pursue them. If you *did* register the copyright, it will be a lot easier to pursue them because now you are entitled to attorney's fees if they lose. You might be able to just write them a letter that says, "Excuse me sir, you are using my copyright, and I am entitled to attorney's fees if we do have to go to court over this. You may want to reconsider what you are doing and pay me for the time or the work that I did for you." So make sure you register your copyrights. The fee is only

$35, and you can register your copyrights at copyright.gov. If you want a step-by-step guide on how to register your copyright and trademark applications visit our resource center at Black-WallStreet.com.

Legal Pillar Recap - Part 1 and Part 2

Incorporation: First, we discussed whether you should be incorporated as a separate business entity or not. I want you to remember that *you* are not your business. You cannot dip into your business bank account and use the money as if it's your own. Your business entity should either be located in your home state or in a state like Nevada that has charging order protections and tax benefits. We also discussed how to protect your personal assets from your business assets and/or your business activities and how to avoid guaranteeing anything personally.

Agreements: We discussed why you need agreements. I gave you a new way to think about agreements and a method to create your own simple agreements without an attorney. We then discussed how to hire new team members, protect yourself from these team members, and what to do if you need to fire them. We also discussed how to protect your brand.

By now, you should be completely ready to step into your business from a legal perspective in a whole new way. Make sure that you head over to the members' section at BlackWallStreet.com with any questions that you might have, and remember, commit yourself to taking action now!

Action Steps:

Write down the agreements that you know you need to document in your business that have not yet been done.

1.

2.

3.

4.

5.

6.

Do you need a standard client agreement? Are there agreements with vendors that have not been documented? Do you need an independent contractor agreement with those independent contractors that are working with you? Write it down and commit yourself to setting up these agreements as quickly as possible because if they are hanging over your head it will minimize the way you put yourself out there in the world. It will shrink the way that you show up in the world and in your business because deep down inside, you know that you haven't dealt with this issue.

Write down the names of everybody on your **team** right now:

1.

2.

3.

4.

5.

6.

If you are unsure about employees versus independent contractors and have people working for you, go through our checklist at BlackWallStreet.com and make sure that your employees are employees, and your independent contractors are independent contractors. If you do have independent contractors, make sure you have independent contractor agreements in place. If you don't, add "put my independent contractor agreements in place" to your things-to-do list. And last but not least, do some writing about your brand. What is your brand? What do people know you for, and is there something you need to register, either a copyright or an actual trademark?

Write your thoughts and action steps down now:

_____

_____

_____

_____

If you need additional resources on brand strategy and development, consider purchasing our companion workbook at BlackWallStreet.com. In the next chapter we will discuss insurance, what insurance you need, what insurance you don't need, and how much it should cost you.

THE INSURANCE PILLAR

Congratulations! You have now reached the second pillar of the **Black Wall Street LIFT Foundation**, which was designed to **LIFT** your business up to ultimate success. Now it's time to discuss insurance. The number one reason why people do not have insurance is the cost. In this section, we give you the tools to evaluate what you need and don't need, as well as how to find the right insurance advisors for your business. Insurance is about empowerment and has nothing to do with fear. You need to know that you have the right insurance in place so that if something happens in the future, you will not have to pay out of pocket for it, and at the same time, you will be able to compensate someone who deserves to be compensated. Things happen in life. That is just the way things are. You want to make sure that you have the right systems set up and the right structure set up, so you are protected when things do happen. Insurance is about sending a message to yourself that says, "I care about you," and it really is your first line of defense when something does happen. Insurance is not just about paying out a claim; it's also about covering any legal bills that you may have in defending a claim. No matter what, even if you do have the right legal foundation in place, you can still be sued. Anybody can sue you at any time for anything. Insurance will cover the cost of a lawsuit if you are sued. And that is a huge peace of mind. My client didn't have that in place when their employee sued them, and they ended up settling their lawsuit for a small five-figure settlement simply because they could not afford to pay the legal fees to defend that claim. A huge contrast to my other client, who left a company to start their own business then was immediately sued by their former employer. Their lawsuit went on for several years to the tune of $2 million. But because they had insurance, the right kind of insurance, they were able to cover all of their legal expenses. Today, that company is a successful, thriving, multimillion-dollar business of its own. If they did not have insurance, they probably would have had to go out of business.

Let's talk about how to determine what kind of insurance you need for your business. The first thing you want to determine is what to insure. **You should insure three things–your home, your business, and your life.** One person who you definitely need to have on your team of business advisors is an insurance advisor. It might even be more than one insurance advisor because there are so many different types of insurance. Your home is different from your business, and your life, of course, is different from your home and your business. Bottom line, what you really need to find is an insurance advisor who is not just an order taker. An **order taker** is someone who will quote you prices then give you exactly what it is that you asked for. Order takers are the reason why so many people end up with the wrong type of insurance. Let me be clear. Some of the best salespeople go into the insurance business because they have such a high commission product. You really need to be careful that you don't end up with the "salesperson" insurance advisor because they will sell you things you don't need. I see this all the time when I am servicing my clients, especially with one particular insurance company. These guys are some of the best salespeople in the world, and they were selling people all types of permanent-type life insurance with high commissions that people really didn't need, under the disguise of tax savings and investments. Eventually, I had to stop working with this company because even though they brought me a lot of clients, I didn't feel good about what they were selling. This is not the type of insurance professional you want either. What you are looking for is a trusted advisor, someone who will really get to know you, get to know your family, and get to know your business. You want someone who will ask you questions like, "What is your plan for your business? What is your growth strategy? And what is your exit strategy? What is your long-term vision? Where are you going with your business?" Once your insurance advisor really understands your life, your business, and the vision you have for your life and your business, then and only then are they equipped to tailor an insurance proposal to your specific situation and needs. Now they will be able to give you some options that you can and should choose from. Again, business is a team sport. I strongly suggest that you take this proposal to your personal business lawyer and ask them, "Does this plan seem like a good idea to you? What do you think about this? Which of these plans would you choose for me?" Again, try to find an attorney that offers some type of monthly membership so they are not charging you hourly or a flat fee every time you want to contact them; have that attorney review the proposal with you and help you make the right decision from an objective standpoint.

Insurance falls into three major categories. Your home and personal property is one category. Your business is another category, and then your life insurance would be a third category. So let's discuss your personal insurance first. What you insure with your personal insurance are your home and your personal assets. If you own your home, this is called a **homeowner's insurance policy**. If you rent your home, this is called a **renter's insurance policy.** These will cover anything that goes wrong in your home, including somebody getting hurt, losing property, or having something stolen from your home. There is also something called **valuable articles insurance**. If you have any valuable articles like jewelry, artwork, priceless heirlooms, anything of that nature, you may want to get a quote for valuable articles insurance. This is extra insurance over what your renters or your homeowner's insurance policy may cover.

You may also need to have automobile coverage. This is your personal property, and if your automobile is not owned by your business, this will be covered by you personally. If your automobile is owned by your business, then it should be covered through your business. The key here is to make sure that you also have an **uninsured** or **underinsured motorist policy**. Often, people waive it to save money, but this is not the place you want to save money. There are just too many people out here today who do not have insurance, and of course, these are the people who will likely get into an accident with you. Surprise! They don't have insurance, so that means you have to pay for everything out of your own pocket. But if you have underinsured motorist or uninsured motorist coverage, the insurance policy will take care of this for you. Again, this is not a place you want to be cheap.

Another thing you should consider on the personal insurance side of things is an **umbrella insurance policy**. An umbrella policy is exactly what it sounds like. Close your eyes and imagine a big umbrella that covers everything. You have your home, automobiles, priceless heirlooms, everything you own, and any potential liability coverage. An Umbrella policy extends the liability coverage you currently have on your homeowners, renters, and auto policies. Your umbrella policy may cover things like slip and falls in your home, a car accident, or identity theft. If you ever have a judgment against you that is in excess of the liability limits of your standard policies, your umbrella policy would kick in and pick up the difference. More often than not, to get an umbrella policy, your homeowners, renters, and your auto policy must all be in the same place for the company to be willing to quote you, so you should definitely talk to your insurance professional first. You should also consider a **commercial umbrella policy** for your business to cover any claims in excess of your business insurance or even your personal umbrella. These are all awesome things to talk with your insurance advisor about on the personal side.

So, what types of insurance do you need to put in place on the business side? There are several types of business insurance policies that you should look into. The first is **general liability insurance.** This will cover you for anything that might happen with respect to your business, other than incidences related to you providing your services. For instance, one of your employees does something, or one of your employees sues you, or you have someone get hurt on your property. Anything that happens in your business due to its interactions in the world, excluding the provision of your services, would be covered by this policy. For example, if you are a coach, a therapist, a lawyer, a dentist or chiropractor, any of these types of businesses, you need to have a separate kind of liability insurance called **Errors & Omissions** or **Professional Malpractice** coverage. These cover any act that goes wrong in the provision of your services–things that will not be covered by your general liability insurance policy. So remember, if you are a professional service provider and you are providing a service, you need to have two different kinds of insurance: general liability and errors and omissions or malpractice coverage. You need both. These are not the same thing. One will cover you if something goes wrong in the provision of your services, and the other will cover you if someone gets hurt in your business, outside of the provision of your services.

Now, if you really want to have comprehensive coverage, you should also ask for **Employment Practices Liability Insurance**. You need to specifically ask for it because it is generally not covered by your general liability policy. Employment practices liability insurance is typically a little bit more expensive, but it is absolutely worth it.

Find out how much it is and how much extra it will be to have this covered. Ask questions like, "What does it cover? Does it only cover discrimination, or does it also cover, for example, wage and hour violations?" Your general liability coverage will cover you if one of your employees gets hurt or if they sue you for something other than employment practices. If they sue you for your employment practices (this is what my client was sued for - employee wage and hour violations because she was not keeping good records of employee break times and overtime), you will not be covered unless you have employment practices coverage. If my client had employment practices liability coverage, then the insurance would have covered the lawsuit against her and covered her legal bills and court costs to defend that lawsuit. If you have team members who work for you as employees or even independent contractors, this is definitely something you want to consider. If you have a team, you want to make sure that any losses by that team against you for your employment practices will be covered. You need to conduct your own cost/benefit analysis to determine whether or not that is a good investment for you and your business.

You may also need **Buy-Sell Insurance**, also known as **Key Man Insurance**. If you have a partner in your business and one of you wants to exit the business someday, then you want to have an agreement called a **Buy-Sell Agreement**. You may recall the buy-sell agreement from the **Black Wall Street Legal LIFT Pillar** in the last section. We are discussing it again because you need to make sure that the buy-sell agreement is funded by buy-sell insurance (Key Man Insurance). Anytime you are in a partnership or multi-owner business, you really should have a buy-sell agreement. The buy-sell agreement will say that in the event that one of you dies, the survivor is going to buy out the family of the person who died for the value of the business. You need this buyout to be funded. Otherwise, where would the survivors come up with the money to buy out the business from the family of the person who died? With buy-sell insurance or a key man policy, the company's founders or owners are insured by the company, so the company pays for the insurance. Then, in the event a partner dies, the insurance proceeds will come into the business to be used to continue operating the business or be used to fund the buy-sell agreement and allow the surviving partner to buy out the surviving family members of the person who passed away.

If you are a solo practitioner, you need to consider what will happen to your business in the event of your death. Will your family have enough operating capital necessary to keep the business going? Have you set things up in a way so that the business could continue to run so your family can sell it? Do you have systems in place? Are these systems documented? Do you have a succession plan in place? This is something you should discuss with your trusted advisory team, including your business lawyer, to help you put this plan in place. Just make sure you are thinking about these things in the beginning and planning these things out. If you are building a business that will be a legacy for your family, you want that legacy to be a legacy of love and ease and not a big fat mess for them to deal with after you are dead and gone. Buy-sell insurance or key man insurance is one of the ways to ensure that the business can continue to run by giving it the liquidity necessary to run, even if you are not here to run it.

Whenever you are considering insurance, be sure to read the fine print. You need to have clarity on exactly what your policy will cover. If you do not have this clarity on what your policy covers, please write a note in an email or a letter to your insurance advisor so they can clarify. You should state, "Based on our conversation, here's what I understand my policy to cover. If I don't hear from you within the next week, I will assume this is correct." Make sure you memorialize exactly what your insurance will cover so that you are very clear on this moving forward. Always, always, always document your understandings with your insurance advisor. Because if you wait until something happens and your policy does not cover what you thought it did, by then, it will be too late. You need to document these understandings in writing *before* something happens. And listen, this is one of those hard conversations you do not want to have because it might make you look stupid, but you know what they say, "There is no such thing as a stupid question." So make sure you get clear on the details. Ask the hard questions and have the hard conversations. This is what it means to be a boss.

Now let's talk about workers' compensation. **Workers' Compensation** will cover your employees' injuries if they are hurt on the job while working for you. Many people think they do not need workers' compensation because they do not have employees, and all of their team members are independent contractors. Business owners beware. You may have designated them as independent contractors, and you may be paying them as independent contractors, but in reality, they might not be independent contractors. For instance, what if something happens and they try to get reclassified because they want to be compensated for an injury, or want to receive employment disability or receive unemployment insurance? If they have been laid off, the government might reclassify them as an employee. If they get reclassified and are injured, and you do not have workers' compensation, that could be a really big problem for you. If you think that your independent contractor might actually be an employee, you should talk with your lawyer about this. You can certainly go through the test offered in our companion course at BlackWallStreet.com to determine if this person is an employee or an independent contractor. Again, it is important because you will always be the one on the hook if anything goes wrong. It may be in your best interest to get workers' compensation. At the very least, you should get a quote so you know what the cost looks like. If it's just a few hundred dollars a year, then you may want to get it just to save yourself the headache.

Another very important insurance to have, especially if you are self-employed, is **disability insurance**. If you own your own business, you are definitely self-employed. Here is the long and short of disability insurance. If you get disability insurance, you need to get a private-pay policy. It's much more expensive than a group policy, but it is also much better. Why do you need disability insurance? One in five people have a chance of becoming disabled in their lifetime. That is 20%. If you don't have disability insurance in place and you lose your ability to work, you have no way to replace your income. Disability insurance replaces that income. Disability insurance will cover your income in the event you cannot work. As I said before, there are two types of policies—**Private Pay** and **Group**. **Private pay** is more expensive, and it's paid with after-tax dollars.

In comparison, **group pay** is less expensive and paid for with pre-tax dollars. Group policies typically require you to be 100% disabled, which is a very high standard. What they really do is reduce the benefits that you would otherwise receive from social security income. Private pay will supplement those benefits. If you are looking at disability insurance policies, it is very important to understand what you get. Make sure you look for language that says the insurance company has the discretion to determine the benefits. *This is language* *you do not want to see.* So let me just repeat that. **You *do not* want to see language that says the insurance company has the discretion to determine benefits or see a definition of disability that pays only if you can't perform each and every material duty of your occupation.** If you have a policy like this, it is not a good policy. What you want is something that says you are disabled if you are only able to perform one or two duties of your occupation. **You also don't want to see language that indicates you are only insured if you are unable to do your own occupation for a period of at least two years.** Make sure you look at and understand the length of time you have to be disabled in order for the insurance to kick in. You also want to make sure that the policy protects your income level as your income fluctuates. You do not want to be locked into a lower income than you were at the time that you become disabled. Your income will increase as you and your business grow, and you want to be sure that the policy benefits will increase too. You should also understand how these benefits are paid. Benefits are usually paid based on what you are paying yourself through your business. If you are paying yourself a thousand dollars a month through your business and that is your salary, and you are running all your expenses through your business, when you go on disability, guess what? Your income is based on a thousand dollars a month, not on all those expenses that you were running through your business. So you need to really think about what the income is that you are showing on your taxes because that is what your disability insurance will be based on.

Now let's look at some of the common conditions that could be excluded. These are things like chronic fatigue syndrome, fibromyalgia, and a herniated disc. You need to look for a list of these things in your policy because if this is one of the things you are concerned about or have had experience with it in your family or in your health during your lifetime, that might not be the right policy for you. So you want to make sure you pay attention to the list of excluded illnesses.

You may also want to consider **short-term disability insurance** versus **long-term disability insurance**; long-term disability could have you waiting a period of at least several months. You need to make sure you know what the waiting period is. If it's a long time, you might want to think about filling in with some type of short-term disability coverage. And remember, you can always self-fund your own disability insurance. What does that mean? It means that you set aside money every week, every month, or every quarter so that in the event you do become disabled, you will be able to fund your own time of inability to work using your own savings. That is the other thing to think about, at least for the short term, but that is probably not going to be enough to cover long-term disability unless you've got your business to a point where if you did become disabled, you could sell your business to fund the rest of your life without working.

Health Insurance

Health insurance is a big issue for those of us who are self-employed because often we worry about not getting or having enough coverage. What I urge you to consider is a health savings plan. A **health savings account** is a high deductible insurance policy. The deductible amount, let's say it's about $5,000, is going to be the same amount that you can set aside pretax dollars into a bank account called a health savings account so that when you do need to use your insurance and pay that deductible, there's money in this account that can be used to pay the deductible. And that money is pre-tax dollars.

So let's say my deductible is $5,000. Each year, I can put approximately $5,000 into a health savings account, and I don't have to pay taxes on that money. Right there, that saves me 25% to 35%. Now it's just sitting there in the health savings account to cover medical expenses. If you have to go to the doctor, buy eyeglasses, anything dental, or anything medically related, you can use the money in your health savings account, like a couple of years ago when one of my best friend's son broke his elbow and needed surgery. She needed the whole deductible, so she was able to go into the health savings account and pay for his medical bills. The really exciting thing is that if you don't use the money in your health savings account, it stays there, and it rolls over from year to year. It continues to earn interest during that time. It does not incur any taxes on earnings. It just sits there building up. It is your money to continue to use for medical expenses whenever you may need them. This is particularly good for me because it keeps my insurance costs down, and I do not go to a doctor very often anyway. It actually encourages me to look for alternative remedies. This is how I discovered preventative medicines, which by the way, I can pay for out of my health savings account if I choose to do so. Your health savings account covers many things not covered by insurance–like chiropractic, naturopathic, and all of the holistic modalities. You can pay for this out of your health savings account if you choose to do so, but you could also pay for the expense out of your own pocket and allow the health savings account to continue to grow tax-free over time. So that is something everyone should look into instead of a traditional, regular low-deductible type of policy, which can be very expensive. You also want to look into a group policy for your company, as well as some individual policies. As long as you are insurable, an individual policy can be much less expensive than a group policy. The downside of an individual policy is that if you have a health crisis, you may end up uninsurable. With a group policy, you can't be uninsurable. They must ensure you as long as you are part of the group.

Life Insurance

Now let's talk about life insurance. **Life insurance** is about making things as easy as possible for your loved ones should anything happen to you. I hear a lot of people say they do not believe in life insurance. Let me be clear. Life insurance is not something you believe or don't believe in. It is something that you invest in for your family's benefit in the event something happens to you, to give them liquidity so that they will have enough assets to live on when you are no longer here. If you don't have any children who are dependent on you, and if you don't have a spouse who is dependent on you, then maybe all you need is enough insurance to cover the end of your life issues–things like burial, cremation, or as we talked about earlier, maybe to fund your business so that it can continue on without you until it is possibly sold. You really only need life insurance if you have people or a business that are depending on you. If your business would really be okay without you, and you don't have any dependents, then maybe you don't need life insurance.

Another thing to note about life insurance is that there are a lot of unarmed black men killed in the black community. The film, *Black Friday,* produced by one of my clients, Ric Mathis, speaks about life insurance as a way to transfer wealth and to deter the unnecessary killing of unarmed black men, women, and children. How can life insurance do this? Because when people die with life insurance, the insurance company steps in to not only just pay the family, but they will also defend or pursue litigation for wrongful death actions to recoup their losses. Then you will have insurance companies who will also have a vested interest in black lives. This is a definite financial and economic way to make Black Lives Matter.

I want to talk about two major types of life insurance–**term insurance** and **permanent insurance**. There are many different types of permanent insurance, which we will get to in a minute. The vast majority of people will only need term insurance. Term insurance lasts for a certain period of time–10, 20, or 30 years depending on the policy, and the amount you pay does not increase. You pay for term insurance every year, and at the end of that term, if you have not died, the money you paid in is gone and the insurance company wins. Maybe you really won because you are still alive, but you no longer have any insurance when the term ends. In some cases, you can get term insurance that is convertible into a permanent insurance policy. That will typically be a little more expensive, but it could be worth it if you are concerned that you need permanent insurance and you can't afford it right now. **Permanent insurance** is the kind of insurance you will have in place no matter what, and it is much more expensive. Part of your payment is paying into the insurance, and part is building up cash value.

Now remember, life insurance people are sales agents. The salesperson types are going to sell you these policies and tell you it's a good investment. I can always tell you that permanent insurance is usually not a good investment. Permanent insurance is really great if you know that you will need permanent insurance when you die. There are three situations where you actually do need permanent insurance. Number one, you may want permanent life insurance if you have an estate tax situation where your family will have to pay estate taxes at your death, or you want to replace the 50% of your assets that might go to the government to make sure that your family has the benefit of all the assets you are leaving behind. You can make up this difference or pay the estate tax with insurance. If you have estate tax issues, please make sure that you are working with a very good attorney who will help you identify whether insurance is the right way to go or whether there are other strategies that you can use to decrease your estate tax because you will need to pay the premiums on that insurance policy. If you are deciding to use insurance to cover estate taxes, you need to have what is called an **irrevocable life insurance trust**. This will ensure that the insurance is outside of your estate for estate tax purposes and will not simply become another taxable asset.

The second scenario where you will need permanent life insurance is if you have a child who will always be dependent on you–a special needs child, or if you have a stay-at-home spouse who will never go back to work in the workforce. This was the case for one of my elderly clients. She was married to a successful plumber, and she ended up living a lot longer than anybody thought that she would. By the time she died there was no insurance, and they lived through much of their savings from him selling his plumbing business. Today, that elderly woman lives on a fixed income and really has to count her pennies, something that she never thought that she would have to do in her eighties. This is true for a lot of elderly women. They live in poverty or near poverty because their husbands died before them, and they are not left with enough assets or insurance to take care of them for the rest of their lives, especially as women are starting to live longer.

The third situation where you should consider permanent life insurance is to ensure that your business has liquidity in the event of your death. Another one of my clients purchased term life insurance when she was 28 years old. She purchased a million-dollar policy that cost her $330 a year. When she turned 31 and went back to get another million-dollar policy, the insurance doubled in price, so she ended up getting another half a million-dollar policy at $450 a year. The reason that she desired to have a $1.5 million life insurance policy was because she was the breadwinner in her family. She had two children and wanted to ensure that in the event of her death, the $1.5 million would be able to go into an account for them, and their guardians would be able to use the interest on this account to make sure that all of their bills were covered. And when they are old enough, they will be able to have access to the $1.5 million to start their lives, pay for college, and/or start a business. This was the number that felt right to her. She felt like the interest would replace the income that she brought into the family and be enough for them to live on and do the types of things that she would like them to be able to do throughout their lifetime. When you are considering how much insurance you need, it really is specific to you and your family.

As a rule of thumb, always get as much insurance as you can afford. You don't want to get so much that it affects your lifestyle today, and at the same time, you really want to realistically look at what you would want your family (spouse and children) to be able to do if you are not here. You should seek to replace your income, and you should try to replace your income with the interest on the insurance – not the principal. The estimated 5% safe interest rate or better should be your goal. For example, on a $1 million policy, if you take a million dollars and put it in the bank at a rate of 5%, you will earn $50,000 a year. If you want $75,000, then you will need a $1.5 million policy. If you wanted $100,000 in income, that would be a $2 million insurance policy. That would allow you to have those incomes from the interest payments without going into the principal. This is why you have to look at it from your own family's perspective. Again, this is where you would get your insurance advisor and your personal business lawyer involved to help you make this decision. Make sure that the person who's helping you make this decision is not paid on commission only if you buy. If this is the case, also bring someone along who is not paid on commission to give you a third, unbiased professional opinion.

We should also discuss estate planning because it really does tie into the insurance discussion. **Estate planning** is insurance for your family. It's about making things as easy as possible for your family after you are gone, whether through incapacity or death. If you have children, the number one most important thing you must do is name guardians for your children, both personal guardians and financial guardians. If you have not named guardians for your children yet, immediately head over to BlackWallStreet.com and name guardians for your children. You will find free resources to help you do this on our website. If you have already named legal guardians for your children, you may still want to go to this website and make sure you haven't made any of the six common mistakes that most parents make when they are choosing guardians–so that if you made any of these mistakes, you can fix them right away. You should also make sure that you name financial guardians and set up a trust for your children. Any life insurance you have should not be payable to your children directly but should be payable to the trust you set up for them. The trust should be the beneficiary of your life insurance policy, and the financial guardians will be the trustee of the trust to take care of the money for your children until they are ready to receive it. I cannot stress this enough. You do not want your children to be the beneficiaries of life insurance. If children are the beneficiaries, the court will have to get involved and appoint a financial guardian to watch over that money for your children until they are 18 years of age. This, of course, is something that happens only if the children are incapacitated or are under the age of 18. This can be very expensive, time consuming, and very public. You do not want to put your family through something like this. Make sure you set up a trust and have the trust be the beneficiary of your life insurance proceeds.

So that is insurance in a nutshell. What you should remember is that insurance is your first line of defense. We covered how you can put the strongest possible foundation beneath your business using insurance and how insurance is not something to be afraid of. It is really about being empowered and doing the right thing for your business and for yourself. You can never stop anybody from suing you, but you can ensure that you have the right financial resources to deal with the lawsuit effectively by having insurance in place. Insurance is really the gift you give to yourself to not have to stress and worry about your life and business. You will not have to worry that somebody may sue you. You will not have to worry about a disability, and you will not have to worry about dying because you know that your business and your family will be taken care of. We discussed the different types of personal and business insurance and how to determine what types of insurance you need. We also talked about why you need an insurance advisor and what kind of insurance advisor to look for.

Action Steps:

List all of the insurance coverage you have right now, including the amounts, and list all possible insurance types that you may need to add. Do that below.

1.

2.

3.

4.

5.

6.

List all the possible insurances you need in addition here:

1.

2.

3.

4.

5.

6.

Now that you know exactly what you need to do to fill any holes in your **Black Wall Street LIFT Foundation** when it comes to insurance, do that now before you go on to the next chapter. And if you want step-by-step guidelines on how to do that, make sure you check out our resource center at BlackWallStreet.com.

THE FINANCE PILLAR

This chapter is about the financial systems that underpin every successful business. As you recall, we are building a business with a strong foundation made up of the four pillars of Legal, Insurance, Finance, and Tax so you can pursue your highest vision without worry, doubt, or fear. We have already covered the legal pillar, as well as the insurance pillar. Now, let's talk about the Financial Pillar. Financial systems are one of the most important pillars and maybe one of my favorites, being that I am TheWallStreetLawyer.com. In the Finance Pillar, we make sure you completely understand how the financial systems in your business can be used as a crystal ball to see into the future and make the right decisions, critical decisions, with the benefit of knowing what will come when you do make those decisions down the road. When you have these financial systems in place, it will clarify a lot of things for you in your business.

The Finance Pillar is all about financial freedom. In this chapter, we focus on helping you avoid expensive finance mistakes. After you complete this section, it is my hope and desire that you will view your numbers in an entirely new way. You will see them as a crystal ball that will allow you to see into and predict the future, and help you stop sabotaging yourself and your business. With this awareness, you will begin to take personal responsibility for everything that happens in your business. You will build the components of a rock-solid financial foundation that will ultimately set you financially free. Truth be told, a lot of people are held hostage by financial fear. It is the kind of fear that keeps them up at night, which keeps them from focusing on high-income producing activities in their business, the kind of fear that keeps them from being present with their family and even being present in their own lives. If you can manage to get freedom from financial fear, you are 75% of the way towards ultimate freedom. That is how important this particular pillar is because I am willing to bet that if you are like most business owners, your financial fear may be driving a lot of the decisions you are making in your business and in life. Whenever you are operating from a place of fear, you can't possibly be operating in the world at your highest level. It is only by living through that fear and dealing with it head-on that you will be able to bring awareness to that fear and receive liberation. A liberation that is your God given birthright.

Your business is all about the numbers, and these numbers will never lie to you. So many of us, and I say us, myself included, bury our heads in the sand when it comes to the numbers. This is what I did in the past, but not anymore. Operating that way costs too much money, and it definitely will cost you your peace of mind. We are entrepreneurs. We are creative. We are excited. We are salespeople. We are marketers, and we are service providers. Dynamic service providers. We just want to go out there and do our thing to make a real difference in the world without worrying about the financial part of it. Knowing and understanding what financial systems you need and how simple it can be to create them will be very liberating for you and your business.

The first thing you must understand in the finance pillar is that the answers to all of your questions are in the numbers. You should be looking at your numbers regularly, and you need to know what you are looking at. You must understand what your numbers tell you. Yes, you read that correctly. Numbers tell a story, and you must be able to understand what that story is. The story the numbers tell is the difference between a real business and an imaginary business. Do you recall my definition of an imaginary business? There are many business owners out there today who have what I call an imaginary business. And it's not just me who calls them imaginary businesses. The IRS calls them imaginary businesses too. If you have an imaginary business, the IRS will reclassify your business as a hobby because it is not really bringing in income. An imaginary business looks good on the internet. It has a fabulous web presence, and it appears that it is doing wonderful things in the world and helping a lot of people, but its bank account begs to differ. The business is imaginary. There are nonprofit businesses that only exist to do good in the world and not make money–they do not have huge income coming in other than what is needed for the necessities; payroll, etc. But this is probably not you. The number one purpose of your business is to make a profit. If your business does not make a profit, it is not sustainable. Your business must earn money, and if it doesn't make money, it doesn't make sense.

Making your business profitable can be extremely stressful and lead to emotional family issues that may block your ability to make money, even when you "do the right things." With the world as it is today, I believe internal conflict is something we all must deal with in one way or another. So how do you deal with it? The section on the laws of the universe presented you with tools and resources to help you get energetically aligned with the income that you deserve to receive because life is meant to be abundant. And when we say abundant, we mean abundance in all areas of your life. So pay attention if you feel any type of resistance, stress, or even disbelief as you go through and set up your financial systems for success because this is a huge red flag. I can tell you that working on the emotional side of wealth, doing things like creating a vision board, acknowledging my talents, and owning my self-worth have definitely been activities that affected my financial bottom line. Learning to accept that I was in business to make money was one of the biggest lessons that I had to go through. When I finally realized that I was in business to make money, and not just enough money to get by, but real money, everything in my business began to change. That is when I finally took my business to a million dollars a year in revenue. I was finally willing to ask for what I was worth, and I learned how to say "no," to people who did not want to pay me what I was worth. Like I said before, getting in right alignment with my worth was the real journey.

As a black woman in America, my self-worth is under constant attack. I have always fought back ferociously for my own value because I am my first line of defense. Listen carefully. You have to fight for yourself and your business in this world. You must assert your God-given right to be here. This is what ultimately got me looking at my numbers, which allowed me to bring in higher numbers in my business, much more than before. The way that I managed my finances at the beginning of my business went something like this. I would look at my bank account, and I would see if there was money in it. If I had enough money in my bank account, I would spend it. I suspect that many of you out there are managing your finances in the exact same way. Once I understood what numbers I needed to look at in my business from a financial perspective, using the **Black Wall Street LIFT Finance Pillar**, it really gave me a framework to begin to see my numbers in a whole new way. This is the framework that I will teach you in this chapter, giving you exactly what you need to know to become a successful business owner with Supreme Awareness. It will save you years of stress, heartache, and pain. And at the end of it all, once you implement what I am sharing with you in this chapter, you will have a real business that you can count on no matter what. You will have the faith of knowing that you will never run out of money. You will know that all of your needs will be met in every single moment. It's a wonderful feeling to know that no matter what happens, you, your family, and your business will survive. Not just survive but thrive! So how do you get there?

I cannot stress this point enough. I got here spiritually before I ever saw any changes in my bank account. This is why you should really pay attention to everything that I discussed in the chapters on the laws of the universe. My first step was to focus on getting my spirit and my soul in right alignment with the abundance of the universe (through healing, growth, visualization, and the law of attraction), which allowed me to be open to all the ways the universe could provide. That is when I was introduced to Alexis Neely and the **LIFT** foundation that I am sharing with you in this book. So you cannot negate the spiritual work. I believe the spiritual work that you do is the most important piece of the puzzle. Remember, the outer physical world you manifest is merely an example of your inner world, just as much as a healthy tree is the outward physical manifestation of the healthy roots of that same tree. *As above so below, as within so without.*

The financial pillar is not just about looking at your numbers. It's about putting you in a position where you can have confidence in yourself and what you do, which will impact how you show up in the world. The first thing you must understand about this pillar is that this is not something you can do alone. It definitely takes a team unless you are a natural finance person. A natural finance professional who looks at their numbers all the time using spreadsheets. And you already have your bookkeeping system set up and are looking at reports every month and know exactly what you are looking at. A finance professional who makes all of their investment decisions based on these reports. This is not the majority of people, so don't feel bad if this is not you. Most people need a team. One of the biggest things that every entrepreneur must come to terms with is that this team will cost money. You have to spend money to make money. This is the place where you definitely want to make a good investment. Most entrepreneurs understand investing in their business from a marketing perspective. Most of you know that you have to spend money on marketing to bring in clients. What you don't realize is that it also costs money to keep your money, and that you have to spend money on team members who can help you watch your numbers. I thought this was something that I should be able to do alone. In the early days of business, it was something that I could do alone. Today you have QuickBooks to help you with your books, and they even allow you to pay a little extra to have someone to do the bookkeeping for you who is a part of the QuickBooks team. But again, QuickBooks is an investment, and having an additional person do the bookkeeping is another investment. This is the place where you do not want to be cheap and cut corners. I can promise you that it will cost you more to fix things after the fact if you do not get the right team in place from the very beginning.

I talk a lot about my mentor, Alexis Martin Neely, throughout this book. She did not have the right team in place in her very first business. Ultimately, that business had to close down, even after it was sold. She sold the business for pennies on the dollar of what it was worth because she didn't have the right financial systems in place. Not to mention the man who bought her business was not able to continue operating it. It all came down to her not having the right financial team in place, and as a result, when she attracted a buyer, she attracted a buyer who did not have enough financial ability in place either. She didn't know enough to look at his background to see what he had going on behind the scenes. The truth is, all of that was a symptom of her hiding and not wanting to look at her financials head-on. Today, she works with an amazing financial team that she talks about all the time. What is so great about this financial team? They help her see her numbers with clarity. She now knows how to look at her numbers. She knows what she's looking at, and she also knows what she's *supposed* to be looking at. She uses these numbers to predict the future, which allows her to make decisions that are not based on financial fear. That is what she taught me, and that is what we are going to learn about in this chapter.

The very first financial team member you need is a **bookkeeper**. If you are just starting out, I highly recommend using QuickBooks for your bookkeeping. It is not expensive, and you can pay a little extra to have a live bookkeeper help you create the revenue streams that we will talk about later in this chapter. Just know that you need to have a bookkeeper. This is a key role to fill. I do not want you doing your own books. With today's technology, you can open a business checking account, and the bank will issue you a business debit card–you can and should make all of your business purchases on your business debit card. In and of itself, that is a great way to do some record keeping on what money you are actually spending on your business. You don't have to enter in receipts manually anymore (Thank God). Today you can simply look at your bank statements to determine how much money you spent on your business, as long as you made all purchases with your business debit card. You should still hire a bookkeeper as soon as you can–even if you have to pay for it out of your own pocket. You need to have your financial systems set up very early on, and you can hire someone to set that up for you in QuickBooks. You can pay them as needed instead of having them on the payroll, but you do need to consult with someone. Your bookkeeper is the person who will help you chart your accounts that are in your financial bookkeeping system. Your **chart of accounts** is where all of these receipts get entered into from your bank account, which shows your income and expenses. And with QuickBooks, you can actually link your business bank account to your QuickBooks account and import all of your data. All of this can and should be set up right from the very beginning. If you do not have your chart of accounts set up from the beginning, it will be a bit confusing to get cleared up later on down the line. A good bookkeeper takes the time to understand your business, because they cannot create the correct chart of accounts if they do not understand the specifics of your business. They should ask questions like, "What are your various sources of income, and what are your standard expenses?"

I didn't realize how important that was until I helped one of my serial entrepreneur clients set up a logistics business. I sat down with his chart of accounts and began to look at his profit and loss statements and soon realized there was no way we could track anything because none of it made sense. When I compared his QuickBooks reports to his actual bank account and what he actually spent money on, I realized I couldn't even look at his QuickBooks chart of accounts because it really did not show me where he was spending his money. Having QuickBooks means nothing if your chart of accounts is not set up the right way. You need to be able to take a look and say, "Here are all my various income sources," and have them broken out separately so you can see which revenue stream brings in a lot of income and which one does not. You can then determine whether or not you should put marketing behind that particular revenue stream. You may decide that another revenue stream is not bringing in any income, but it is where all of your expenses are coming from so maybe you should delete it. You will be able to make decisions from an educated perspective. It allows you to make the kind of decisions that only can be made if income and expenses are being coded properly throughout the process. If they are not, the reports that you get will be completely meaningless to you. Again, this is why you need to sit down with a bookkeeper at the very beginning.

I remember spending three whole days with my bookkeeper after my business was already up and running to restructure the entire chart of accounts. It was a big, cumbersome job, and then I had to go back and code all of our income and expenses so that they made sense for us. You may even find yourself doing this once a year when you are trying to determine your income and expenses at tax time. That is how I used to do things. When I first started my law firm, I would stress out during tax season preparing my books for my accountant because I was not charting these things properly throughout the year. Today, I get really meaningful, timely reports. I see which businesses I want to continue, which I do not, which services I want to continue to provide, which I do not, which products I want to continue to offer, and those I do not, all from a financial perspective. To get the reports that you need, reports that actually help you make these important decisions, you need to have your books set up the right way. That is what your bookkeeper will help you do.

So let's talk about In the Black Resources, LLC, for example. We have our 6-week **Black Wall Street LIFT Your Black Business Building Course** that we sell for $2,500 online at BlackWallStreet.com. Periodically, about three times a year, we discount it to $1250. We know exactly when those promotions will happen, and we sell a certain number–let's just say we sell about one hundred. Now we can plug that number into our projections. When those months of the year roll around, we can ask ourselves, "Did we hit our numbers? Did we make our projections?" We also have another three (3) month coaching program called Black Wall Street Businesses Accelerator Program for entrepreneurs that we sell for about $5,000. Based on these numbers, I make projections based on things we are going to sell–and let's say we sell about a hundred of these. In hindsight, I can ask, "Did we meet our numbers?" With our **Black Wall Street Corporate Counsel Program**, we know we offer open enrollment periodically throughout the year. We have the down payments that come in at that time and then the monthly membership dues, so we make these projections. The key is to separate all of these income sources rather than just have all of the income that comes in lumped into one category.

With my law firm, I have separate streams of revenue. I have estate planning revenue, and within the estate planning revenue, that is broken down into our **Black Wall Street Family Plan**, our **Black Wall Street Trust Plan**, our **Black Wall Street Wealth Plan**, and each has different price points $2,000, $3000 to $5,000, and maybe even $4,000 to $6,000 to $8,000, and I can do projections. I think we're going to do about ten trust plans this month, and based on that, this is how much income we can expect. I also have business planning that has a certain expected income. So the more that you know about your business, the more you can separate these income sources. You will want to separate them to track how you are doing and what you are going to do. Then you will want to do the same thing for your expenses.

There are two different types of expenses—fixed expenses and variable expenses. **Fixed expenses** are expenses that you know you will have to pay every single month, no matter how much income you bring in. Payroll is a fixed expense. You might also have variable expenses, which include things that will change depending on, in my case, the case and the client at that time. For example, in my law firm, I have variable expenses like filing fees that vary from state to state and different filing fees from case to case. I know that every time I sign up a client to start a business for them or to incorporate their company or file their litigation lawsuit, I will have to pay a person $300 for service of process. I may have to engage a person and pay them $500 to type this up. I may have to pay someone $300 in filing fees with the department of state. A **variable expense** is an expense that varies, such as overtime. You want to categorize all of these expenses and break them down so that you can track and ask yourself, "How am I doing? Am I spending more than I thought I would? Am I bringing in more money than I thought I would? Am I bringing in the money that I should?" This tracking system will be able to identify where you are in the process of making money in your business.

Now, another team member you should consider at some point, especially in the beginning, is the **Chief Financial Officer** or the **CFO**. Now I know that you think CFOs are only for big corporations, which would not make sense for your small business, but you're wrong. Take your business seriously, even if it's just in the beginning. Have a CFO come in on a virtual basis to help you set up your financial model. I've worked with outsourced CFOs frequently, and what they will do is build the basic financial model for your business. A **financial model** will show all of the various expense streams you can expect, and your variable expenses. An experienced CFO will show you what you should expect and help you understand your expenses. It's especially helpful if that CFO worked in your industry before. This financial model really becomes the first financial budget for your business.

To be honest with you, I hate the word budget. It's not really my style. It feels a bit restrictive. So I like to think of it more as a **spending plan**. Just as much as the word "diet" sounds restrictive, and instead of diet, you would just say "a healthy way of eating." It's more about awareness. Supreme Awareness. This spending plan financial model will bring awareness to your business. It's a guideline–an expectation. For example, if you expect to receive $5,000 from a certain source, and it ends up being less, you weren't necessarily wrong. It just means you have to look at what happened and adjust the expectation. What caused you to miss the mark? Do you need to make a shift in your marketing? Do you need to adjust your pricing? Again, it's simply a point of awareness. It does not mean that you are a failure. It just means that you didn't know something–that you were unclear. Now that you have actual real-world experience to compare it to, you have more knowledge. You have more clarity, and next time, you will be a lot clearer. What is really important is that it's going to tell you when you can make investments in something and when you cannot, and how you should price your services.

I am going to give you a little example of how not having this hurt me. When I started my law firm, I was very busy but successful. I decided to bring in other lawyers to work with me so that I wouldn't have to see all the new clients on my own. This was my growth strategy, but I didn't want to pay the other attorneys a salary. I decided that I would bring them in as independent contractors, and I made a deal that I would give them 50% of the clients they engaged. If they engaged a client at $4,000, they would get $2,000. They thought that sounded great. We moved forward with this agreement, but it turned out I was losing money. I did not know that my profit margin on my services was only 30%, and I was giving 50% away. I didn't know my numbers. I now work with a CFO, but back then, I just picked this number out of thin air because it seemed like a fair split. This was an expensive lesson to learn. I don't want to see you make these kinds of expensive mistakes. I want to see you run your business the right way from the very beginning. If that means that you need to work with a CFO, even on a very short-term basis to get your first financial model set up, do it! And then, your bookkeeper can provide you with a monthly profit and loss statement that will let you know if there's any variance, any difference between what was on the actual profit and loss statement and what was on the financial model. Then you can have a conversation with your bookkeeper or with your team and ask, "Why was there a difference? What can we do to hit those numbers? If we went way over, great! How can we use the extra resources to support the growth of the company?" Looking at your numbers this way is ultimately how you begin to predict the future. You take this financial model and create a baseline for comparison. Then every month, when you receive your profit and loss statement, you compare it to the financial model.

The other thing that your CFO can do for you is forecast a rolling budget for six months to a year into the future. You will be able to say that if things are continuing the way they are, your business will be well paid or out of cash. If you don't figure this out until it's happening, it will be too late because you will not be able to do anything about it at that point. Remember my client who made their first million dollars then got hit that following April with a hundred-thousand-dollar tax bill they were not prepared for? When they found out, they had to go to the bank and get a loan. Luckily, they had a great relationship with the bank and they could get the loan, but imagine if things were different. You need to have foresight. What will happen if you continue on this trajectory? What you can begin to do is have some backups in place. You can get a line of credit to support the growth of your business or get a loan while you still have time to do so. This is why many companies go out of business. They run out of money to pay their bills because they didn't anticipate the problem. There always has to be a safety net.

Financial Reports

Let's look at what reports you should be looking at on a monthly basis. The first one is your **profit and loss statement**. The profit and loss statement will show all the various sources of your income, hopefully, broken down by various sources instead of just one big lump. It will also show you all the expenses broken down by category. As I said before, you want to match this up with your projections, and you need to get this from your bookkeeper 15 days after the close of each month–30 days at most. If your bookkeeper is not getting you this within that time frame, you need to find a new bookkeeper. This is another sign that I didn't see. I was not given this report on a timely basis in my first business. I didn't know how important it was. The next report that you should be taking a look at on a regular basis is your accounts receivable report. Your **accounts receivable report** tells you who owes you money and the status of their accounts. If you have anyone that makes payment plans or is on an ongoing payment schedule and not paying you all upfront, you need to know who they are, how much they owe, and for how long. You need to take action as quickly as possible when someone owes you money. The longer you wait, the lower your chances are of collecting. An accounts receivable report will help you stay on top of that. Your **balance sheet** is a snapshot. It's a quick picture of where you are right now. How much money do you have in the bank? What are your other assets? What are your other liabilities? You need to take a look at this every month just to see where you are now in relation to where you want to be.

You should also be looking at your general ledger. Your **general ledger** will be a list of all the checks that were written and all of the bills that were paid, especially if you have someone else writing these checks for you. This is another reminder of the importance of having a solid team. Your team members will be checks and balances for one another. I have a personal assistant. He knows everything about me. He does everything for me. He keeps an eye on the bookkeeper and our virtual CFO. He works with me every month to look at what the bookkeeper and CFO are doing to make sure that everything is done in the right way and that nothing funny is going on behind my back. Ultimately, I oversee every person in my business. If I am not watching them closely, I guarantee you somebody will fail to do their job effectively. That is just what it is, and that is what it means to be a boss. From hiring to firing and everything in between, you want to run your business from the perspective of a business owner with Supreme Awareness.

If you are avoiding something, your eyes are closed, and your head is buried in the sand. You're not looking at it, and this is where you are going to have trouble. This is just the way the universe works. Tackle the problem head-on and fix it. I talk a lot about turning problems into opportunities and the reason why we are allowed to endure adversity. I remember having this conversation with God after I got on the other side of my adversity. "You know, God, I mastered turning problems into opportunities. When will I get to a place in my life where I can get some of my opportunities and blessings the easy way?" What came to me next was a message from Rev. Dr. Michael Beckwith. He was on Oprah's show talking about his new book, *Life Visioning*. He said, "Life will stop kicking you into gear once you get into gear voluntarily." I'm paraphrasing, but you know deep within your heart and soul where you want to be. Deep within your imagination you can see the biggest, boldest, and brightest possible future for yourself. If you want life to stop pushing you around and pushing you in that direction, you should get in harmony and align with that vision as soon as possible. We should always run our business from this perspective of Supreme Awareness. Aware of our greatness. Aware of our power. Aware of our possibility. And we should constantly be moving in that direction.

Credit

Let's talk a little bit about credit. Credit is a key lifeline for business owners–here is why. When you have a line of credit supporting your business, it allows you to take bigger risks, and you have to be able to take risks to grow your business–plain and simple. There will be times in your business when it's time to grow, and you will need to make hiring decisions and investment decisions before you have the revenue to support it. This is what growth is all about. It is about spending money before you have it. It's about jumping off the ledge, taking a leap of faith, and saying, "I am serious about my business! I am going to make these investments into my business." To make these investments and feel okay about them, you need to have sufficient capital behind you. There are important things that you should know about credit. We will talk about business credit versus personal credit in a minute, but first, I want to stress the importance of having relationships with financial partners.

Credit is one way to borrow money to grow your business, and having an investor is another. I know many people think that only bad people need to borrow money and that you should be able to finance your business with your own revenue streams. I thought this too for the greater part of my career, but the mentorship, leadership, and guidance from my investor and business partner is why I am able to bring BlackWallStreet.com to you today. So you never want to close your mind and heart to opportunity. Just make sure you can bootstrap your business and build it until an angel investor comes along.

When you pitch your first investor, remember to make your request bigger than you think it should be. As we say on Wall Street, "Go Big or Go Home!" Do not hold yourself back by playing small. Just make sure you can back up your request with numbers. The key to getting enough money is having a solid business plan in place. This is what is going to make credit possible for you. And you want to be able to show lenders your business plan. Make sure you do it with energy and excitement! How can you expect someone else to be excited about your business if you are not excited about your business? Business is a team sport. Do not think that you have to go at it alone. Think about it. Go into your dentist's office, and you will see all of those extra chairs and computers in his thriving business. Do you think he really did that on his own? Of course not. Most likely, he did it with other people's money. They financed him because he believed in himself enough to ask for the money he needed to grow his business.

Now it's time to discuss **business credit** versus **personal credit** because there absolutely is a right way and a wrong way to use credit to finance your business. Most business owners are financing their businesses with their personal credit cards. When you finance your business with your own personal credit card, you are making it more difficult for you to start over if something goes wrong with your current business. Why? Because you are hurting your personal credit score. If you have more than 30% of your credit used, your personal credit score goes down, and guess what? It makes it harder to get a business credit score. If you finance your business using your business credit and then go out of business or ultimately cannot pay your bills and max out your business credit line, it does not hurt your personal credit score. You do need to have a high personal credit score to build business credit. Once you build business credit and use your business credit to finance your business, it does not impact your personal credit score.

If you decide that your business isn't working and is going to go out of business, it doesn't mean that you failed. It just means that you are learning. You will have a much easier time starting up business number two or three if your personal credit score is still intact. Keep in mind, you will likely need to have a personal credit score above 675 to get business credit. If you don't, you might need to find someone to partner with, but first, check out the resources that we have for you at BlackWallStreet.com to see if we can help. Even if you have a score lower than 675, the key is to focus on your business credit instead of your personal credit. In the early days of your business you may have to use your personal credit. Just try not to use it to such levels that it will hurt your personal credit score. And remember, we have all the tools you will need at BlackWallStreet.com.

I know we discussed the importance of not guaranteeing things personally in the legal section and making sure you are not personally guaranteeing anything on behalf of your business, but this is slightly different. Make sure you are using business credit when you are financing things on behalf of your business, and make sure you spread your debt out among various cards so that you are lower than 30% usage on all your credit cards if you have to use your personal credit. Whenever you are getting business loans, make sure you apply for them in the name of your business and use your business credit whenever possible.

Here is the key to all of this. Your financial systems are going to set you up for success. If your financial systems are not set up in the right way now, even if you are avoiding it, you must address this first and foremost. You can't beat the financial system set up. It will be harder to do the longer you wait. The sooner you just bite the bullet and say, "I am going to start taking my business seriously. I am going to set up my financial systems. I will take the first step and I will do it now," the easier and better it will be for you in the long run. The hardest part is getting started.

Action Steps:

Run a google search for bookkeepers, pick up the phone and start interviewing bookkeepers. List your potential choices and their fees here:

1.

2.

3.

4.

5.

6.

Run a google search for virtual CFOs. Pick up the phone and start interviewing Chief Financial Officers. List your potential choices and their fees here:

1.

2.

3.

4.

5.

6.

Start researching banks for your line of credit. List the potential banks right here:

1.

2.

3.

4.

5.

6.

You do not need to do everything all at once, but you do need to get started. If you are already in the six-figure revenue range to the high six-figure revenue range, it is very critical for you to do this. If you are in the five-figure revenue range, do it now. **It will be so much easier for you to do it now.** If you already have a seven-figure business and haven't done it, get on the phone with a CFO ASAP. You might be saying, "How can this be? How could someone with a seven-figure business not have the right financial systems in place?" Easy. This is a business that is great at bringing in money, not so great at managing it. This was the case for my client who sold their business for much less than it was worth to someone who ultimately couldn't make a success of it because he didn't have the financial knowledge to do so. The new owner eventually stopped paying the bills and ran out of money. This never has to happen to you. Your financial team is the key. **Hire a CFO. Hire a bookkeeper. Make the investment. Get the line of credit.** It really is that simple.

Your business is always about the numbers. You are in business to make money and to turn a profit for you and your business partners. Yes, you are in business to provide the service that you provide while also making a huge difference in the world, but your business cannot do this if it is not making money. Without money, it can't pay its payroll, it can't pay its rent, it can't pay its suppliers, its vendors, and ultimately, it can't pay you. This is why the Finance Pillar is the most critical of all the pillars. You cannot do this alone. You need the team we have talked about.

To recap, you need a bookkeeper (and/or QuickBooks). You need to work with a CFO at least virtually or part-time, maybe more, and you need to be analyzing your profit and loss statements, your balance sheets, your accounts receivables, your general ledger, and comparing these reports against the financial model that your CFO set up for you regularly. You should also be using your business credit and not your personal credit cards. Go to BlackWallStreet.com, where we have a lot of great resources on how to hire a bookkeeper, how to hire a CFO and a number of other credit resources. Dive in and start wherever you need to. Just start. That is the key.

THE TAX PILLAR

Throughout this book, we have been discovering how to **LIFT** your black business by building a strong foundation made of the four pillars of Legal, Insurance, Finance, and Tax beneath your business so you can pursue the highest vision for your business without worry, doubt, or fear and follow the path and mission of your soul. Now we're going to talk about the fourth pillar, the Tax Pillar. I know this is scary for many of us, so we will break it down, so you see there is nothing to fear. In this chapter, we will discuss what tax planning is and why it is so essential for wealth building. We will discover key deductions that you could be missing and what to do if you are audited. Our systems will help you take the fear out of the audit. Then, of course, we will help you set up your tax system for success.

Remember, having a solid **Black Wall Street LIFT Foundation** in your business is what shows how serious you are about your business to your clients, your vendors, your referral sources, your family, lenders, investors, and everyone that you know. It will literally affect how you and your business show up in the world. That is why you are here. We are here to help you build a meaningful business that can withstand the test of time because, ultimately, that is what you really want and need. At BlackWallStreet.com, we are all about helping you

142

become a real seven-figure multimillion-dollar business owner. That's what this is all about—at least a multi thousand-dollar business owner. My goal with this book and course is to take the fear and mystery out of it for you, and with taxes, there can be a lot of fear and mystery, which is why you need to have professional advice. But just because you are getting professional advice does not mean you don't need to know what you need to know as well. You need to know how to hire the right CPA—someone who is not just a just a tax preparer but also helps you make projections. You need to have at least two meetings a year. You should have one around the September/October timeframe to do some projections for the end of the year, and then you need to have one right after tax time in the summer to look into some of the strategic things you should be doing going forward. At the very least, you need to have one before the end of the year while there is ample time to take action before tax season.

Most CPAs have this cookie-cutter approach. They treat every client the same. They are only concerned about getting your taxes filed. And this cost my client a lot of money. As you remember, I keep talking about what happened when I coached my first client to earn a million dollars. She had a very surprising $100,000 tax bill–tax bill that could have been cut in half if she actually knew about it ahead of time. We learned a very valuable lesson that year. You need to know what to ask your CPA. You also want to know what to look out for on your tax return before you sign it. I want to give you a fabulous resource on taxes. It's a book called *Lower Your Taxes - Big Time,* by Sandy Botkin. It's a great resource–it's a big book, but it's a really easy read. If you apply what you read, you will save a huge amount of money. In the Tax Pillar, we do a big overview of what is important and what you need to know in regard to your taxes. But here's the thing that you must first understand. I am not a CPA, tax professional, or accountant, and you definitely need to work with them. I am sharing with you some of my own trial and error experiences and mistakes, along with those of a few of my clients, so that you can learn from our experiences. I am also going to share with you some of the things that you may be overlooking. As we covered in the last chapter, your CPA should be working very closely with your bookkeeper. Your bookkeeper should be working directly with your CPA to make sure that things are categorized correctly in your **chart of accounts** so that you can take maximum advantage of the **tax deductions**. The question I want you to ask yourself is: **How can you live the corporate lifestyle so that you can deduct far more than you are deducting right now?**

What exactly is the corporate lifestyle? Taxes are your greatest expense, and tax planning is the last great tax shelter that exists. It's legal, and what's really great is that if you do it right, it will lead you to wealth even if you are not making a huge amount of money. As I mentioned earlier, taxes are your greatest expense. In fact, your tax bill can exceed everything you pay for food, shelter, transportation, and clothing combined if you add it up with all the state and social security taxes that you pay. If you can decrease your taxes, you are going to keep a lot more money. You can actually get rich by just reducing your tax expenses and investing the money that you save. Most people do not do it this way because it feels complicated and confusing, and they don't know what to do. No one wants to get in trouble with Uncle Sam, so what do they do? Usually, most people do nothing. Most people ignore it and avoid it because this seems to be the easiest way. It's really not the easier way, and I hope by now you've seen that. I hope you understand this because we are the Black

Bulls of Wall Street, and we are Big Business Owners. We tackle our problems head-on like a BOSS!

Think about how much less hard work you will have to do to be wealthy if you reduce your taxes, invest that money, and let your money grow for you. You won't have to make a lot of money because your money will be working for you without you having to work for it. Reducing your taxes is a fantastic way for you to multiply your efforts. Remember, when you add up all the taxes you are paying, it can sometimes exceed 50% of your income if you do not do things the right way. That is a lot of wasted effort and money because the number one reason to have a business is the tax savings. If you have a business and you are not taking advantage of the tax savings, then you are missing out on one of the biggest advantages to owning a business.

America was built on capitalism. Thus, we have a number of loopholes in the tax code for people who are out there creating businesses and building enterprises in pursuit of the American Dream. The reason business owners get tax breaks from the IRS is because they know entrepreneurship drives everything! Job creation, poverty alleviation, and American innovation. More businesses mean more jobs, which is better for the economy. If you are an employee right now and don't have a business, let this be the wake-up call that inspires you to start your own business, even if it is only for the tax savings. In fact, did you know that your legitimate business deductions can exceed your income, and you can use business losses to offset the other income you have? No one wants to have a loss. You are in business to make a profit. However, if you did have a loss it can offset other income, and you can deduct a lot of things that you are probably paying full price for right now when you start to **live the corporate lifestyle.**

There are two tax systems out there—one for people who get W-2 wage statements and *do not* know the tax rules. Then there is one for the self-employed people like us, business owners who *do* know the rules. The tax system is like a game, and if you know the rules, you can win the game. If you do not know how to play, you could lose the game. I can tell you that when I worked for a nonprofit company at the beginning of my legal career, I earned about $60,000/yr. At the end of the day, I felt like I did not have any money. When I started my own law firm after I lost my job and relied only on my law firm for income, I made the same amount of money, but I felt richer. I felt like I had more money because my business was paying for so many of the things that I used to pay for myself personally.

The first thing you need to know is that you will be taxed on income received from all sources. Whenever you receive income from anywhere, you are taxed on that income. This is referred to as your **gross income**. You can deduct many expenses from your gross income. And as I mentioned earlier, if your deductible expenses exceed your income, you have a tax loss that can be applied against other income. If you do not have other income, that tax loss can be carried forward for a certain number of years to be applied to future income. If you are a sole proprietor, there is another important thing you should know. You are five to seven times more likely to be audited than a properly incorporated business. This is because you file your taxes differently when you are a sole proprietor than when you have your own business. As a sole proprietor, you file your taxes on your personal return on what's called your Schedule C. When you have a separate business entity that has been set up the right way, you do not file your taxes on your personal return. You file a whole separate tax return, and your business gives you a K-1 that shows you what needs to be filed on your personal returns. So remember, when you have a separate business entity there are two separate tax returns. When the government sees that schedule C, you become five to seven times more likely to be audited. It is still a possibility that one day you will be audited by the IRS even if you have a business entity, but if you keep good records, you will have nothing to worry about. The goal is to have your business viewed by the IRS as a *no change*. A no change means that you will not owe any more in taxes to the IRS.

Deductions

What deductions should you take, and how do you take them? If you set things up the right way in your business, you can deduct everything from entertainment to medical expenses to your children's education. Now you may say, "How can I do this? How can I do these things the right way?" This is where the games begin. It all depends on how you set things up in the beginning and how you maintain your business affairs over time. If you have not already done so, I strongly urge you to get our companion course that goes with this book at BlackWallStreet.com. I do a deep dive where I talk specifically about how to properly take business deductions. Let's talk about a couple of those things here.

I've already touched on **living the corporate lifestyle.** From now on, every time you go out to dinner or go to an entertainment function, treat it as a business meal or a business event. Make sure that you bring business partners or colleagues and talk about your business before, after, or during the entertainment or the meal. It *does* need to have a business purpose, and you *do* need to keep track of it in case you are audited. One of the first things you'll do after reading this book is to begin keeping a **tax diary.** This tax diary is a simple calendar where you notate money spent on business related activities. Every time you eat a meal or attend an event write down the answers to five questions. You need to do this right on the receipt so you can keep it in your tax diary or simply add the receipt to your diary next to your written answers.

Questions to ask are: *Who? What? When? Where? and Why?*

Who was the meal with?
What did you talk about?
Where was it?
When was it?
Why did you have it?

Then you take this receipt from this event, and you put it in the pocket of your tax diary just in case you get audited. Thank God it's 2020. If you are paying for everything on your corporate debit card, you should have a record of it in your business bank account and your bank statements forever and ever, amen. Just make sure you keep a diary that has a date, and you list your five W's: *who, what, when, where,* and *why.* If you do this every time you have a meal, every time you go to a sporting event, every time you go to a nightclub or a golf course or have a party at your home, you can deduct the expense and make yourself audit-proof. Remember, keeping accurate records keeps that shield of protection around your business.

Home-Based Businesses

What if you have a home-based business? I heard a rumor that home-based businesses are being audited more than they have in the past, but I do think this is just a rumor. Especially in the age of the internet. Should you have a home-based business? What are the benefits? Look at all the things right now that you are buying for your home that are really for your business. Your computer, printer, paper, printer's ink, pens, notebooks, or maybe you have a water machine or something like that. Maybe your office is part of the cleaning for your home if you have a home-based business, a gardener, all of these things that you would buy anyway for your home, now can become business expenses that can be deducted off of your income when you have a home-based business. This is why you should consider bringing your business home and maximizing some of these deductions.

Vacations

Now let's discuss vacations. How can you turn your vacation into a tax-deductible event? Make sure you never take another vacation again where you are not doing some sort of business. I know what you're thinking. *I don't want to do business on my vacations!* But I want you to change your thinking–and here's how. What if every time you took a vacation you gave a seminar, or you entertained potential business partners or clients? Keep track of it and write it in your tax diary. Make your vacation a business event. Why do you think people have seminars on cruises? I taught my first CLE (continuing legal education) course on a cruise and got CLE credit for it with the state bars of Texas and New York. I actually received double credit because I was in attendance and teaching, which covered my CLE requirements for the next two years. I must say, it was also one of the best vacations that I ever had. I did the Michael Jackson *Thriller* dance. I swam in blue water and fed the fish. It was really fun. You should also be thinking about these things creatively. How can you make your next vacation a business event? One of my favorite clients is a spiritual healer and teacher of a specific method of meditation, and she wanted to go to Africa. She booked a couple of events there, and now she is on vacation and on business in Africa while writing the whole thing off. Of course, she's making a lot of money while she's there, which is really nice as well. You can do that too.

Children on Payroll

Should you pay your children? Yes! You should definitely have your children on payroll! I have a client who paid $50,000 for her kid's private school education. Guess how much money she had to earn to pay $50,000? She had to earn $100,000 because it was taxed close to 50%. After taxes, she had $50,000 left to pay tuition. These are after-tax dollars that she was spending on education. What could she have done instead? She could have "hired" her kids. She could find things for them to do and paid them each $25,000, which is obviously a lot easier to do if you have older kids. Let me be clear here - you can't just hire them to pay them. You must have legitimate work for them to do. Maybe you could use them for modeling. Maybe you are using them in advertising. What would you pay for a model? What would you pay an actor? You can even do this with little kids. You can pay them $5,000 a year, and then they can put that money into an IRA account or retirement account that will grow tax-free. If they are a child, they may not have to pay taxes. If this is an option for you, I recommend at least paying them a little bit so they can start putting it into a retirement account. This is a good way for you to maximize the shifting of income in your family. This is how you keep more money in your family. Your children will need that money one day, maybe to pay for school or start a business, and that will take the burden off of you. If you do this, you need to keep great records of what your children actually did and what you paid them for. This is also a great way to teach them about money and how to have a job by really giving them an actual job. I think this is one of the best reasons to be in business—to involve your children and family in the business and teach them how to build wealth as a family. You know what they say, "A family that plays together stays together."

Medical Expenses

Medical expenses are not normally deductible until they exceed 7.5% of your AGI (adjusted gross income). That is typically a lot of medical expenses before the deductible, but if you are a business owner, you can do a number of other things. You can set up a medical reimbursement plan, which will allow you to deduct all of the medical expenses that are not covered by your insurance. You may want to think about hiring your spouse if you are married, and you would need to pay someone to set it up, but it's worth every penny. If you have full-time employees, you have to cover all of your full-time employees with your medical reimbursement plan. This is a great strategy if you have a business that doesn't have a lot of employees and you want to keep those employees happy.

Last but not least, we need to talk about how to prepare for your meeting with your CPA.

As I mentioned earlier, you should meet with your CPA at least twice a year. Summer is a good time, then close to the end of the year so you can do your projections and prepare for tax season.

Questions to ask your CPA:

1. What will my tax situation look like next year?

2. What can I do right now to reduce my taxes?

3. What are some tax strategies that I can put in place at this point to lower my taxes?

4. What red flags do you see?

Pay close attention to the breakdown of your taxes, specifically where it breaks down the expenses of your business on your return. You should always look for red flags on your return. We do a whole webinar in our companion course where we discuss some of these red flags. Make sure you watch that webinar to understand the details of your tax returns to know exactly what you are looking at before you ever sign another return.

So what do you do if you get audited? Remember, the auditor is a person just like you, and that auditor has a huge amount of discretion. You must also realize that they are extremely busy. If you treat the auditor with kindness and respect your audit will go a lot easier, so don't take everything personally. This is why I highly recommend that you turn your audit over to a trusted person like your CPA. It may cost you a little bit of money to have someone do this, but it's worth it. You want to look at an audit as a challenge, as an opportunity for you to step into a higher version of yourself. It is not about you, personally. You are not being attacked, and you don't have to feel guilt and shame. Go into it realizing that you are being tested to determine how clear you are about your purpose, how clear you are about the path you are on, and whether it is all worth it. If your answer is "Yes," then recommit to setting up your business the right way. Remember, problems are opportunities in disguise. This is an opportunity to become a stronger person and a stronger business owner. This audit is a new opportunity to give you a new perspective that you did not have before. This is how you must always look at challenges. Most people retreat. But not you. **You are armed with the law of adversity, and knowledge is power.** With your new perspective, you will look at that problem and say to yourself, "Wow, what a gift this is! And I am going to use this gift to become a better version of myself!" And that is what our **Black Wall Street LIFT System** is all about. It's about **LIFT**ing your business to a higher level and opening your consciousness and awareness to the money-making decisions, business decisions, corporate decisions, and hiring decisions that will always positively affect your financial bottom line. You begin to walk the blind walk of faith with your business, and you see everything that is brought to you in your reality, good or bad, as a gift. It is a gift for you to learn and grow to another level of who you are meant to be, headed on the right path of where you are trying to go.

Our **Black Wall Street LIFT Tax Pillar** is a little shorter than the other chapters because in this chapter, we have a lot more homework and action steps for you to do on your own. You need to have a CPA to help with tax planning. You should understand why tax planning is so important, how to make the most of your deductions and what to do if you are audited, and how to prepare for a tax audit from the IRS. We discussed the importance of keeping a tax diary. Always, always, always keep a tax diary. Always keep good records with receipts; or better yet, track your spending using your business bank account using the five questions that we touched on earlier: *Who, what, when, where, and why.*

Action Steps:

A. Review the checklist at BlackWallStreet.com regarding the 17 deductions that you may be overlooking. List the deductions that you have been overlooking here:

1.

2.

3.

4.

5.

6.

7.

8.

9.

10.

B. Read the articles on Sales Tax and Payroll Tax at Black-WallStreet.com and write down areas you have been overlooking here:

1.

2.

3.

4.

5.

6.

C. Create a calendar to record all of your deductible expenses daily and keep the receipts in your diary. You can also make these notations on your business bank statements.

D. Watch the webinar on how to look at your tax return in our companion course found in our resource center at BlackWallStreet.com to understand better what you need to be looking at on your tax return.

E. Schedule those two annual meetings with your CPA and your bookkeeper, ideally together, and meet with your business lawyer. Do not wait until March. Do not wait until February. Do not wait until after the first of the year because by then, it will be too late to do some of that strategic and advanced tax planning that you need to take maximum advantage of the tax laws.

F. Start **living the corporate lifestyle**. Open your eyes to the possibilities that are right in front of you. You will save a huge amount of money on your taxes. Do not avoid it just because it's hard. It can be hard to get things set up the right way, but it will feel incredible when you do.

When you know that you are **a serious business owner with Supreme Awareness,** you will start building confidence. You will be willing to charge more for your fees and put yourself out there in a bigger way. You will set clear boundaries, and you will feel great about it thanks to your internal shift. And by the law of attraction, that internal shift is bound to pay you dividends long into the future.

If you've made it this far, you've made it all the way through the system. I want to congratulate you because you do have something to be proud of. You made this investment in yourself, not just the financial investment but a time investment. Most people will invest in this resource, put it on their shelf and look at it every once in a while. It will just be another thing that they are avoiding, but not you. You did not avoid this. You took action, and you moved forward. Go back through and look at the notes you took with respect to each of your action items and continue **moving forward and implementing what you learned into your business!**

Taking action and building your business on a solid **Black Wall Street LIFT Foundation** will strengthen your confidence as a real business owner, and allow you to operate your business from a place of Supreme Awareness.

LEGACY: ESTATE PLANNING AND BEYOND

You did it! You built a legacy you and your family can be proud of. So what's next? One of the biggest considerations you will face as a successful business owner is, *what will you do with the inheritance you created?* How will you preserve your legacy moving forward? Despite knowing how important this is, most people give it little thought. As a result, many families and business owners suffer in court and conflict unnecessarily. The people who are willing to step fully into their own adulthood and make conscious choices about how to leave and/or receive their inheritance can find the process to be deeply healing to the entire family line, honoring the ancestral lineage while deeply serving future generations.

Let me again congratulate you for making it here. You've already taken a much bigger step into conscious creation of life by now addressing what will happen in the event of your death or incapacity. If you have small children, you may consider creating a trust for your life insurance and investment accounts to make sure they have everything they need in case you die too soon. As I discussed in an earlier chapter, you do not want them to get too much before they are mature enough to manage it, so you want to choose someone to handle it for them until they are ready, to make sure they have what they need when they *are ready*. Once your small children become teenagers, depending on the kind of children they are now and how confident (or not) you are about your parenting skills, you may begin thinking about how you can protect what you have accumulated throughout your life for them. Children will grow into adulthood somewhere between totally responsible and completely disabled, and at times, they may pivot between the two. You might also find yourself swinging wildly between totally capable and completely irresponsible with the life you are creating and the legacy you are leaving behind. In most cases, your children will reflect back to you your own fears and your own shortcomings. Regardless of where you find yourself on the spectrum, part of being a mature adult and successful business owner means entering into real consideration about what will happen beyond the short time you are here on earth and how you leave behind the inheritance you created. You may also need to consider how you would receive an inheritance from your parents, care for them in their old age, and create more with what they are leaving you. If you haven't thought about these things, welcome to adulthood. If you are leaving behind an inheritance or preparing yourself to receive an inheritance, and you are planning on creating a will or trust, read the language very carefully. You will most likely see the following:

1. With respect to each share provided for a child of the Grantor then living:

    a. Because each child has attained the age of 25 years, each child shall have the right, by written request, to withdraw one-third in value of the remaining assets of such child's share then being held in trust.

    b. Each child who has attained the age of 30 years, and each remaining child upon attaining such age, shall have the right, by written request, to withdraw one-half in value of the remaining assets then being held in such child's share.

    c. Each child who has attained the age of 35 years, and each remaining child upon attaining such age, shall have the right, by written request, to withdraw the remaining assets then being held in such child's share, and if that child does so withdraw the remaining assets, the Trust as to that share shall terminate.

If you see something like this in a trust, it means that when the **beneficiary** (the person named to receive the trust assets) reaches the age of 35, whatever is left behind through the trust is distributed outright to be put in the beneficiary's personal bank account, and the trust terminates at that point. You may think this is because by the age of 35 a beneficiary should be mature enough to handle the assets being left behind. While that may be true, this is not the best way to leave (or receive) an inheritance.

When a trust terminates, and inherited assets are then put into the beneficiary's personal bank account, these inherited assets become subject to risk from the beneficiary's creditors, from a future divorce of the beneficiary, or from a lawsuit against the beneficiary. Even if none of these things ever become an issue, the beneficiary is not incentivized to grow the inherited family wealth but instead spend it on consumables rather than create with it.

There is a much better way.

Before we discuss a better way, let's look at the five most common ways people lose their inheritance after it is distributed to them outright.

1. Future Divorce

Almost fifty percent (50%) of all marriages end in divorce, and in most divorces, property is divided evenly. While in most cases, property division after marriage does not include an inheritance, this is not the case for inherited assets that are brought into the shared property of the marriage. More often than not, an inheritance received during a marriage is commingled into the marital property and can become subject to division.

For example, let's assume I receive an inheritance of $50,000, and I use that $50,000 as a down payment on a home I share with my spouse. We lived in that home and used marital assets to pay the mortgage. A few years later, we get divorced. In most cases, the full value of that marital home will be considered an asset of the marriage. The inherited assets were absorbed into the marital estate for division upon divorce–inheritance lost.

So if you have a married child, or a child who will get married in the future and you leave them an inheritance and they later divorce, as much as half of their inheritance could go to their ex-spouse in the divorce. If you aren't working as hard as you are to support your child's future ex-spouse, you may want to do something different. You may want to leave behind your inheritance, no matter how small, in a different way to protect what you are leaving from a potential future divorce.

Side note: In some cases, a party can demonstrate to the court that the down payment on the home came from inherited separate property to receive the full value of these proceeds in a property division, but it would cost additional time and money in legal fees to do so. Also, while an inheritance could be protected from divorce with a prenuptial or postnuptial agreement that states the inherited assets do not become part of the marital property, it's far more common that when people marry, they do not want to bring up the consideration of what happens when they divorce. So most people do not get these agreements.

When you leave your assets to your children in a protected (yet accessible to them) trust, which we will discuss below, or you receive your inheritance in a protected manner, you can avoid expensive legal fees as well as the conversation about prenups and postnups altogether and know the inheritance is protected.

2. Mismanagement

According to a study by Professor Jay L. Zagorsky of Ohio State University, 40% of individuals inheriting *less than* $100,000 will spend or lose the entire inheritance, and 18.7 % of individuals who inherit *more than* $100,000 will spend or lose the entire inheritance.

In many cases, inheritors can think about their inheritance as if it were a lottery prize. And lottery winners saved just 16 cents of every dollar won, and bankruptcy rates soared for winners in just three to five years after winning. Why does this happen? Because lottery winners and many inheritors are not properly prepared to receive the money that comes in, and the extra money creates problems they were not well-prepared to handle.

In her book *Beer Money: A Memoir of Privilege and Loss* by Frances Stroh, the would-be inheritor of the Stroh brewing family fortune, Ms. Stroh perfectly illustrates the impact of what happens when junior family members are not properly prepared to receive their inheritance. Stroh tells a story of rampant addiction, mismanagement of the family business, and ultimately loss of the entire $700 million family fortune, which would have been worth $9 billion today. The Stroh family fortune was able to last five generations before mismanagement wiped it out simply because of how much was passed on. A smaller amount of money being left behind would likely have been lost before it could make its way down to the grandchildren.

This is certainly not limited to the ultra-wealthy. Using a trust structure that keeps assets safe while preparing future generations on how to use and manage what's left behind, even when it's not that much, is a key strategic decision that can be the difference between keeping or losing a family's accumulated wealth.

3. Extreme Debt/Bankruptcy

When an inheritance is left outright to a beneficiary, and that beneficiary ends up in extreme debt or bankruptcy, the inheritance is lost. Possible causes of debt include a business venture gone bad, a health event such as addiction, mental illness, accidents, or disease that results in either a temporary or permanent inability to work combined with expensive medical bills, or an accident that results in a judgment, as discussed below.

Extreme debt and bankruptcy do happen to good people, and if you leave an inheritance in a Lifetime Asset Protection Trust, instead of outright, you can ensure that what you leave behind will never be at risk due to a mistake or unexpected health issue.

4. Lawsuit

Unintended neglect that injures someone else's person or property could wipe out an inheritance you leave your children if you distribute your money to them outright.

For example, 2012 ACE Financial Services, Inc. found these lawsuit judgments:

- $49 million judgment in California for an automobile accident where the family of a 21- year-old college student sued drivers of two vehicles involved in the multi-vehicle crash. The plaintiff's counsel claimed one defendant was sleep-deprived while the other was on their cell phone. The plaintiff was in a coma for one month and is expected to require lifetime 24-hour care.

- $20 million judgment in Florida for an ATV accident where a teenage male was killed while riding an ATV on the neighbor's property. The neighbor invited him to drive the ATV, permitting him to operate it without proper safety equipment and without adult supervision. The teenage male struck a fence and was decapitated.

- $11.9 million in Florida for an internet defamation suit brought by a Florida consultant against a Louisiana woman for posting defamatory statements about the plaintiff on an internet bulletin board. The defendant called the plaintiff a "crook" and a "fraud."

- $5.9 million in Maryland in a dog-bite case where a 16-month-old child was attacked and killed by a pit bull kept at the home of a family friend.

In the Florida ATV case, the defendants thought they were doing the neighbor's son an act of kindness by allowing him to have "fun" by driving the four-wheeler around the family property. They didn't tell the young man about the barbed wire on the property. Their good deed was unintended neglect, resulting in the death of their neighbor's son. It was not seen as a good deed by the parents or the court, who ordered the $20 million judgment.

On a smaller level, but just as impactful financially, a friend of mine recently called me because he accidentally left a faucet running at a friend's house where he was visiting. The resulting flood caused $413,000 in damage that the insurance company is now looking to collect. If he had an inheritance disbursed to him outright, it would have been wiped out by this potential claim.

As you can see, well-intended but neglectful behavior on the part of your children, or others around them, could wipe out any inheritance you leave them. If you choose to use a Lifetime Asset Protection Trust to protect what you are leaving behind, an accident won't wipe out the black family wealth you worked hard to create and pass on.

5. Lost Work Ethic

My mentor once said, "Some people can't handle prosperity." He was right. In fact, most people cannot.

For example, Thomas Stanley and William Danko in their book, *The Millionaire Next Door*, uncovered research showing that children who received an inheritance were worth four-fifths less than others in their same profession who did not. Vic Preisser, of the Institute for Preparing Heirs, says that "unprepared children who inherit money are susceptible to excessive spending, identity loss, and guilt over receiving money they didn't earn." According to Preisser, "In a year to 18 months, everything falls apart — marriage, finances — and if there is a drug problem, it becomes worse." The book, *Painfully Rich,* by John Pearson, about the family of J. Paul Getty (who died with $2 Billion to pass on), is very telling. Getty was notoriously frugal, and the way he prepared his children to inherit, or perhaps more notably didn't prepare his children to inherit, caused his children and their children enormous amounts of grief that not only resulted in mismanagement of the money left behind but also mismanagement of their lives.

As you can see, an outright inheritance is NOT the best answer for your children. If you are an heir who might be receiving an inheritance, receiving it outright may sound good, but it really wouldn't be in your best interest.

The Alternative

An alternative to an outright inheritance to your children ("outright" meaning they both personally own and can personally lose the inheritance) is to gift your assets to your children at the time of your death via a Lifetime Asset Protection Trust or to ask your parents to leave whatever they may be leaving you behind in a Lifetime Asset Protection Trust.

A **Lifetime Asset Protection Trust** can be drafted into a regular **Revocable Living Trust** to give your children (or you, if you are the "heir") full control of the inheritance (if you so choose), but at the same time, ensure they never "own" the assets they inherit so those assets would never be at risk of being lost to divorce, lawsuits, creditors or mismanagement.

Because the rule of law is **you can't lose what you never own**, you are gifting your children (or being gifted if you are the heir) with airtight asset protection of the kind they (or you) couldn't give (or create) otherwise at any price. When you leave (or receive) an inheritance via a Lifetime Asset Protection Trust, **the trustee of the trust owns the property**, not the beneficiary of the trust. What that means is that if there is a divorce, a bankruptcy, or a legal judgment, the inheritance cannot be lost. The inheritance is totally protected.

From a management perspective, the Lifetime Asset Protection Trust can be used as a vehicle for education about investing and even business management by allowing the beneficiary to become a co-trustee of the trust with someone you've chosen and trust to support their education and growth. You can even build in provisions to allow your child to become the sole trustee of the trust or the right to become the sole trustee at specific intervals, giving them effective full control without the risk of ownership.

If you are concerned that receiving an inheritance in a Lifetime Asset Protection Trust makes it so that your inheritance wouldn't be available to you or would restrict you in some way, have no fear. Your Lifetime Asset Protection Trust can be structured so that you receive control and access to use the inheritance with no restrictions, so long as you make all investments inside the trust and only take money out of the trust if you would be using it to consume instead of create. All creations could be funded by the trust and therefore remain protected by the trust vehicle.

There are quite a few additional creative ways a Lifetime Asset Protection Trust can be structured so it meets the needs of your unique family. Most importantly, if you are working with the right kind of lawyer, you can use this kind of planning as an opportunity to hold regular family meetings with both older and younger generations to plan for the passage of your family wealth. Here's an important note. Family wealth goes far beyond money. When viewed properly, you can see the money left behind from one generation to the next as a catalyst for family connection, passing on family values, and an opportunity to clarify how the family uses its full TEAM (time, energy, attention, and money) resources.

This is what **Black Wall Street Family Wealth Planning** is really all about. If you would like to learn more about how to build a **Black Wall Street Lifetime Asset Protection Trust** into your plan for what you are leaving behind or what you will receive, schedule a **Black Wall Street Family Wealth Planning Session** at BlackWallStreet.com.

In addition to considering whether a Lifetime Asset Protection Trust makes sense for you and your family, your **Black Wall Street Family Wealth Planning Session** will get you more financially organized, ensure none of your assets are lost to your State Department of

Unclaimed Property, as well as keep your family out of court and out of conflict when something happens to you.

CHAPTER IV

The Laws of Man Mapping Your Path to Freedom: Who Are You?

Abundance is freedom. You are God manifested in human form, and abundance is your birthright. In this chapter, we will be mapping your path to freedom because it is time for you to get honest about what you actually need to earn every month, every week, and every hour to have the life you truly desire. Even if you are well beyond that already, or if you aren't even close, it's very important to know what you need to earn at your minimum level to be thriving at your maximum level to be of service. Once your necessities are outlined, we focus on moving from needs into wants (preferred if you could afford it). In this section, we map that path so you know exactly where to focus your mind, body, and spirit next because this is the key to knowing you will always have enough and feeling fully supported as all of your needs are met. Then you can give back from a place of excess. Remember, our main focus is on your stability, so you never have to make a decision from a place of scarcity, fear, or even greed, which you often can't see. You can't see greed because no one wants to view themselves as greedy. But some of your decisions, if they are not made from a stable foundation, could be being made from that grabby, greedy energy that we want to purge out of your system once and for all.

Now I want to be really clear–this does not mean that you cannot have more abundance. In fact, one of my mentors just had a million-dollar month. You can bet I was cheering right alongside her because I know what she will create with that, who she will help, and that is ultimately what this is all about. We begin with the law of *you,* and **we do that by mapping your path to freedom.**

Here is what we know about the path because it is true of any path. What we know is that when you want to go anywhere, the key is to know where you are now and where you want to go next. If you choose to take the long, scenic route, you really don't need to know exactly where you are going or how to get there because you made the decision that you will start wherever you are and end up wherever the wind blows you. If this is not the place where you are in your life and with your work, then you want to be on the straightest route possible from where you are now to where you want to go. If you just have these vague ideas of what's next for you, you will always be chasing your tail, asking yourself, "How do I get there?"

As you know from your understanding of the laws of the universe, the *how* will always show up when you know *the what*. This is the law of attraction at work. This is why the map is so important. It will show you the straightest path from where you are now to your next destination and your next destination until you get to where it is that you truly want to be. No more escape fantasies. This tool will help you take massive action towards your next step. Get ready to dive into our **Black Wall Street Money Map Workbook**. It's my gift to you. As we said, the first part of your equation is to know what you need. Not a falsely inflated view of what you need but what you really need to thrive at a minimum. Healthy food, a safe, clean place, well cared for children, and opportunities to learn and grow. You might have an intuitive hint about this number, but you need to actually calculate it. Also, note that this number will change, so you will need to revisit it often. Don't assume you know because you calculated it two years ago. I recommend that you update it every quarter, every six months, or at a minimum, every year. And again, this is the essential monthly minimum that you need to earn consistently that will allow your nervous system to truly relax. So you can clarify what to do next. If you are working toward the wrong next, you are going to spend a ridiculous amount of time, energy, and attention, your non-renewable resources in the scramble rather than on taking focused, directed massive action. When you take focused, directed, and massive action, you can achieve the impossible. You might be focusing on getting to your preferred before you have your base or your minimum, or you may be dreaming about no limits before you are even at your preferred. You may be living in that escape fantasy we all have. Mine was moving to a farm. Yours might be living as a nomad or being rescued by a sugar mama or sugar daddy. This could be happening if you are living in an escape fantasy, burned out, overloaded, exhausted, and not using your money to free up time, energy and attention. Whatever it is, we want to eliminate the escape fantasy once and for all.

So, let's get clear. What do you actually need next? We want you to locate yourself on the map. Where is your monthly now, relative to your minimum to be happy? Your minimum to be of service, and your preferred if you could afford it? It is very important to get clear on your now. You are filling out that far-right column so that you actually see the numbers and where you are now.

I want you to notice that I don't talk a lot here about the no limits category. This is for folks who love to dream big. Whatever that looks like, put that into your no limits column. It's important to know where you want to go for the sake of vision, but we don't dwell on this area because it's not really relevant to you taking your next step. What happens if what you need now is less than your minimum? Let's change that up a little bit to make it easier to consider. Let's say that you are living on $2500 a month–that is your now. And let's say that your minimum is $5,000 a month, your absolute minimum to thrive, to have healthy food and the housing situation that really would support your growth and development. If that is the case, then your next level is to get out of survival mode because you are actually in survival mode. You just have to acknowledge that and accept it to be able to get to your next level. What would you do to get out of survival mode? The equation for enough is to ask for what you need in exchange for what you have to give. So, in this case, what would you ask for if your now is less than your minimum? You might need to ask for a job. You might need to ask for a loan. You might need to ask for a gift. Who are you going to ask to help you to get there? Or what are the potential sources of income to get you there? Elizabeth Gilbert wrote the book *Big Magic*. In it she talks about how she took a series of jobs, waitressing and other things that would allow her to earn her minimum, so she wasn't putting any unnecessary financial pressure on her creativity. That might be the situation that you are in. Perhaps you need to take a job that maybe isn't the work that you want to do. You've got to get to your minimum to make decisions from that stable place. This is absolutely critical. If you are not at this very bare minimum, stable place, you will not be able to make decisions because you don't actually have your needs met.

So now your needs are met. Let's imagine that your minimum is $5,000 a month. But what you really need to be of service is $10,000 a month. You're at your minimum to thrive, but you don't yet have the income you need to be able to invest in the support services you would need to truly be of service. You need to focus on using your existing resources to increase your ability to serve and receive more income. Questions to ask include, "What are the investments that you could make, by either increasing the value of your skills, learning how to deliver a new skill, learning how to enroll people in the skill that you have, learning how to package your services at a higher rate, or learning how to get hired more often for the services that you have to offer to get you to that increase of $5000 a month? How can you invest other non-monetary resources (like time) to acquire more? What will earning more allow you to do in terms of increasing the value of your skills or the time that you have to serve? How can you justify making an investment in those skills?

Maybe you need to invest in another team member, or a couple of additional team members, or a coach. How can you justify the investment that you are going to make that will allow you to ask for a loan or ask for a gift? You want to show whoever is making that loan or gift, "Here is where I am now. I am at $5000 a month. I want to get to $10,000 a month. Here is how I am going to invest my time, energy, attention, and money to fill this gap. I need a bridge loan." In the business world, this is called a **bridge loan.** Businessmen and women use them all the time to get from one place to the next. You can leverage and utilize this when you understand what you need, and you have the language to ask for it. It is also referred to as an **investment in working capital.**

In light of the pandemic a common question I receive about working capital is, "How will I be able to use the loan money that I receive from the government in the form of EIDL–the emergency loans that are available because of COVID-19?" These funds must be used for working capital. It should be used to make exactly the leap that we're talking about to close the gap between where you are now and the amount you would need to serve at your next level.

So, what exactly is working capital? **Working capital** is cash that can be utilized to keep the business working. **Initial capital** or **owner equity** is the money you put in to start a business. **Cash flow**, **revenue**, and **income** is what you receive for doing business. As you offer your services and/or your products, you receive revenue or income and cash flow. Working capital is utilized to fill the gap between the timing of income and the payment of expenses. Most businesses require some form of working capital infusions, particularly if they are in a growth phase, or in this case if there's a sharp decrease in business as a result of unforeseen circumstances such as a pandemic. The purpose of these loans from the government, or if you are using business credit, or borrowing from your parents, or using your retirement or savings to make a loan to yourself, is to help the business stay afloat. A bridge loan can pay ongoing expenses while things are playing out in the larger economy or even in your own micro-economy as you are growing your business to the next level. A great number of businesses float working capital in the form of credit card advances, business credit, corporate lines of credit, and trade lines of credit with suppliers. The number one reason that I see people not able to remain in business, even if they have a great service or a great market, is because they do not know how to manage their cash flow and working capital without freaking out. It can be scary if you haven't been taught how to do this. You do not need to shut down the business. As an evolving business you're always going to need a bridge between where you are now and where you want to get to next. So you really want to understand how to work with this capital.

What if your now is *more* than your minimum to be in service but *less* than your preferred? Let's say that your minimum to be in service is $10,000 a month, but your preferred is $25,000 a month. You should now consider the difference between your needs and wants. Do you want to free up time by hiring more support, or do you want to keep more money? Now we're looking at working towards your preferred, which will significantly impact the decisions you make about your income model. At your minimum, you might be delivering a one-to-one service, but you might be maxed out on your ability to deliver that one-to-one service. You're full. Your practice is full. Your business is full. You cannot take on any more clients, but you are only making your minimum to be of service–you are not yet at your preferred. Now you have a choice. How are you going to shift and change your income model in a way that lets you get to your preferred income? That minimum to be of service actually increases because you are bringing on more support. You're not going to take any more money personally. What you need to do is increase the amount of revenue you can bring in, and you are going to use that to hire people until you get to a new minimum to be of service, and then you can start focusing on your preferred.

These are the decisions that you will be making as you get to each of these levels. You want to revisit these numbers consistently, so you are making your decisions from a place of what you actually need and what you want—knowing the difference between those two and managing your time, energy, attention, and money (TEAM resources) intentionally, consciously, and from a place of Supreme Awareness.

If you are at your service level of income but not yet at your preferred, you might need to work more. That work may look like working smarter by bringing on more support to increase your income. It may look like changing your income model and adding additional revenue streams. You will likely need to use working capital to do this because you won't yet have the capacity to serve more people, but you need to increase your income. That means you need to hire more support staff and ask for more help before you have the revenue to justify it. This is why our Black Wall Street **Money Map Workbook** is so vital. It will give you a plan for the revenue and allow you to have the confidence to know, *okay, I can use working capital to bridge from where I am now to where I want to go next.*

If your monthly now is more than your preferred, what you need to consider is what to do with the excess that supports more people in your life and your community. This is where many people who have deeply ingrained scarcity paradigms inherited from the previous generations have a lot of important work to do. If you are earning more than your preferred income and are already living with excess, you need to start looking at how you can live generously in a meaningful way. How can you give what you have to those who don't have as much excess as you do? If you are not already doing that, I want you to start to look at *why?* Where is the insecurity that still exists in your ability to do that? At that point, your ask is going to be, "Who can I help and how? How am I going to help the people in my community? How can I serve?" There is a beautiful book called *Karmic Management.* The companion book with it is a novel called *The Diamond Cutter.* I encourage all of you who are in this place where you are ready to begin giving back to read this. You know your needs are met. You know you have what you want, and now it's about, "Who can I help and how?" How can you create a bigger ecosystem that you and all of the people in your community can rely on?

Your assignment for today is to locate yourself on the map and get really honest about what is your now? What is your next? What is your next task to close the gap? What do you need to do to build the self-trust necessary to make that ask? This will allow you to make an ask not based on a hope, wing, and prayer, but on real numbers, real investments of time, energy, attention, money, (your team resources) so that somebody would feel good about investing in you.

So use our **Black Wall Street Money Map Workbook** so that you are clear on your minimum to thrive, your minimum to be of service, your preferred if you could afford it, and your now, so you can map your next right course of action. Then come share with us in our public group or private membership group at BlackWallStreet.com what your next ask will be because it's very likely that somebody might support you and help you make that ask. I can say that in our **Black Wall Street Membership Programs**, we make all sorts of love matches on our coaching calls. These love matches are situations where one person in the membership has an ask, and another person in the membership steps up and says, "I would love to support you with that. I'd love to give you four free coaching sessions. I'd love to help you get clear on your offer. Or I'd love to give you a job!" That is exactly what's happening at BlackWallStreet.com.

Happy Hunting!

FOOTNOTES

1. Domain Purchase Receipt for BlackWallStreet.com

afternic **GoDaddy**

One Main St
Cambridge, MA 02142
Phone 480-268-8526

Receipt For:

In the Black Resources, LLC
Attn: Marye Dean
30 Wall Street 8th Floor
New York, NY 10005
US (UNITED STATES)

DATE: 7/14/2020
Receipt # blackwallstreet.com

Date	Description	Reference	Amount
7/14/2020	Domain Purchase	blackwallstreet.com	$75,000.00
			-$75,000.00
		Total Due to Afternic	$0.00
		XXXPMXXX Payment	US Wire
		Total Due	$0.00

DOWNLOAD YOUR FREE GIFT

Read This First

Just to say thank you for buying and reading my book, I would like to give you a free gift from BlackWallStreet.com!

#RiseInPower

To Download Now, Visit:

www.BlackWallStreet.com/freegift

I appreciate your interest in my book, and I value your feedback as it helps me improve future versions of this book. I would appreciate it if you could leave your invaluable review on Amazon.com with your feedback. Thank you!